HULL IN THE 1950

A Pictorial Diary
of Life in
Kingston upon Hull

by John E. Smith

With a Foreword by
The Lord Mayor of Kingston upon Hull

Hutton Press
1994

Published by the Hutton Press Ltd.,
130 Canada Drive, Cherry Burton,
Beverley, North Humberside. HU17 7SB

Typeset and printed by
Image Colourprint Ltd.,
Willerby, Hull.

ISBN 1 872167 59 4

CONTENTS

ABOUT THE AUTHOR.

John Smith was born during the 1950s and brought up in the Hull area. He attended Hessle High School and Kingston upon Hull College of Commerce, where he completed a Business Studies course, and later qualified as a Chartered Secretary and Administrator. He is married and for the past four years has lived in Bricknell Avenue.

He spent eight years working at the Jameson Street headquarters of the Hull and East Riding Co-operative Society before joining Hull City Council where he is now employed as an administrator in the Department of Planning and Design.

John has a deep affection for his home city of Kingston upon Hull and has always followed its progress and development with close interest. Since early childhood he has been an avid collector of newspaper cuttings and articles on this topic from which he has compiled numerous scrapbooks. It has long been his desire to use this material as the basis for a chronicle of the events and changes that have occurred in Hull during his lifetime.

This book, illustrated with over 100 photographs, many appearing in print for the first time, is the first step towards realising that ambition. It has a foreword by the Lord Mayor of Kingston upon Hull.

ACKNOWLEDGEMENTS.

In preparing this book I have received valuable help from many people:

Peter Allon, Colin Ashcroft, Steve Betts, Grant Cairns, Eric Cant, Arthur Credland, Jill Crowther (Local Studies Library) and her staff, Geoff Drewery, Brian Dyson, Chris Elton, Colin Green, John Hall, Chris Ketchell, Peter Lawson, Stewart McDonald, David Major, John Munson, John Nesworthy, Geoff Oxley (Hull City Record Office) and his staff, Ian Rogerson, E.J. Russell, Capt. David Saltiel, Steve Shearsmith, Stella Sizer-Simpson, G. Stephenson, Maurice Tarran, Keith Underwood, Mike Wakefield, Les Ward, Steve Watson, Steve Westgate, Julie Withell.

I should like to express my sincere appreciation to them all and indeed to anyone I have inadvertently missed.

My grateful thanks also to the following organisations for allowing me to reproduce their photographs or other material:

Hull City Council: City Record Office, Department of Planning and Design and Town Docks Museum (Harry Cartlidge Collection).

Innes Studios, Hessle (Donald Innes Collection).

Kingston upon Hull City Transport Ltd.

The University of Hull.

The Corporation of the Hull Trinity House.

Royal National Mission to Deep Sea Fishermen.

Messrs. Gelder & Kitchen, Architects.

Sam Allon (Contracts) Ltd. (Sam Allon Collection).

Reckitt & Colman Products Ltd.

BBC Archives.

While every care has been taken to verify the accuracy of the contents of this book, inevitably in a work of this nature, there will be errors and the responsibility for these is mine alone.

J.E. SMITH,
Hull.
1994.

Foreword

By the Lord Mayor of Kingston upon Hull,
Councillor Len Harvey

*The Lord Mayor of Kingston upon Hull,
Councillor Len Harvey.*

While welcoming the constantly increasing amount of local history material in recent times, there appears to be a gap to be filled by a publication devoted to 'Hull in the 1950s'.

Looking around our beautifully laid-out city centre today, it is perhaps difficult to imagine that only forty years ago it lay largely in ruins; our people's homes and lives had been disrupted, sadly in some cases devastated, by the effects of a tragic world war; and a tremendous task of rebirth and reconstruction faced those charged with the administration of civic affairs and the running of our many industrial and commercial concerns.

Despite all they had been through, Hull's people generally entered the 1950s in optimistic mood. National events like the Festival of Britain and the Coronation did much to promote confidence in the future and spread cheerfulness. Apart from all the serious concerns of life that had to be coped with, such as finding a home and a job, there was a great capacity for enjoyment among young and old alike, with theatre, cinema, dancing, sport and other pastimes riding on the crest of a wave. For many it will also be remembered as a time of profound change, with some long-cherished ways of doing things on the verge of disappearing for ever.

In this book John Smith has provided an interesting and highly readable account of life and happenings in Kingston upon Hull during that era. I hope the end product of his research will give pleasure to readers of all age groups and perhaps encourage the further study of what must be regarded as an important and fascinating phase in the development of our great city.

Blundell's Corner in the 1950s. The old paint works remained derelict for many years before eventually being swept away, together with the National Provincial Bank on the corner, to make room for the present Hull Daily Mail building. Photograph by courtesy of Hull City Record Office.

1950

The year that:-

Clement Attlee's Labour Government hung on to power in the General Election with a slim majority.

British soldiers joined forces with 15 other nations in the Korean War; a re-armament programme was introduced.

Home Industry had largely recovered from World War disruption and recaptured 26% of the world market for manufactured goods.

Milk and petrol came off ration.

The first long playing gramophone record was produced.

JANUARY.

1st   With New Year's Day falling on a Sunday, Hull greeted the new decade in a more restrained way than usual. Ships' buzzers on the Humber and the peals of Holy Trinity Church bells broke the silence but the city centre was almost deserted and most people appeared to be celebrating quietly at home.

5th   An unexploded bomb was feared when gardener Bob Richardson discovered a deep hole beneath an elm tree near Hedon Road Maternity Home. The area was roped off with a 'Danger' notice until the bomb disposal squad arrived from Leeds. After digging for some time it was finally concluded that the hole was caused by rotting tree roots and there had been no bomb after all.

6th   Hull's chronic housing problems came nearer to solution at 12.25 p.m. when the Lord Mayor, Alderman John Henson, switched on the power at the new **East Hull Pumping Station** on Hedon Road. The station, designed to raise the flow from the city's newly-constructed deep drains for discharge into the Humber, formed a vital component in the East Hull Main Drainage Scheme. The development of homes and industry on Corporation-owned land had been held up for over twenty years for want of adequate drainage, the situation becoming so serious that the City Council had continued to press the Government for permission to start the scheme right through the war. Work had finally got under way on the river outfall in April 1945 and on a new trunk sewer to Staveley

Road a year later. One of the greatest engineering projects ever tackled locally, it was seen as a turning point in the quest to provide homes for all.

Later the same day about 100 people gathered in Anson Road to watch Commander Harry Pursey MP officially 'open' the first house to be ready for occupation on the **Bilton Grange Estate Extension**. The East Hull MP described the event as as 'a landmark in the history of Hull', bringing new hope to the 13,500 people on the housing list, a third of whom were couples planning to get married. Although work on the estate had started in 1937 and the roads had been laid for some time, the war had caused building operations to be suspended until June 1949. Now there were over 500 homes at various stages of construction with a further 1,500 planned (see page 43).

14th   In Hull's biggest blaze since the 1948 British Cocoa Mills disaster, fire swept through the top floor of corn merchants and cattle food manufacturers Wm. E. Marshall Ltd. in Glasshouse Row injuring three firemen. A man was later charged with arson after telephone wires were found to be disconnected.

17th   Thieves made a £1,200 haul when they entered Alliance Avenue Post Office during the night. The safe was found nearby in Parkfield Drive with cash, savings certificates, postal orders and stamps missing.

19th   Alderman Sydney Smith MP opened a new wing of **Porter Street flats** that had recently been completed by Myton Ltd. The 66 new flats, designed by the City Architect, were the second instalment of a project begun in 1938 and brought the total to 144. Residents were full of praise for the spacious rooms and well-planned kitchens with their generous cupboard space and all-electric, cream-enamel stoves. There was a playground for the children, lockable pram pens, covered cycle racks and an enclosed area for hanging out washing. Weekly rents ranged from 13/5d. for a one-bedroom flat to 19/4d. for three bedrooms. A social hall and shops were also being fitted out on the ground floor. The £112,500 scheme marked the start of a twenty-year plan to transform the densely-packed area bounded by Anlaby Road, Bean Street, Hessle Road and Porter Street into a modern residential 'neighbourhood unit'. Within a stone's throw of the new flats there were houses with no water supply and families sharing a common tap in a courtyard.

27th   After a £3,000 rebuild, Hull's fireboat *'Clara Stark'* was re-commissioned at Charles Pearson's Yard near Albert Dock. The

Brook Street in 1950 showing some well-known shop names that have since passed into history: Bladons, Hicks, Blooms and Thornton-Varley. Bladons were here temporarily until their Prospect Street store was rebuilt. Photograph by courtesy of Hull City Record Office.

At the start of the decade Hull's city centre was littered with ruined buildings from the 1941 blitz. The remains of W.H. Smith's book wholesalers in Jameson Street were cleared during 1950 to make way for the first rebuilding project - Festival House. Photograph by courtesy of Hull City Record Office.

twin-screw boat was named after the wife of Fire Brigade Committee Chairman Alderman Archibald Stark, and played a vital role in protecting 13 miles of docklands and wharves. Demonstrating to the civic party with ten jets in full-flow, she produced an 80 foot arc of water that sent a curtain of spray hundreds of yards down river.

Plans by Parks Superintendent Mr. H. Roscoe to redevelop **Pearson's Park** were approved. The outdated Victorian landscape with paths in all directions so that pram-pushing families could take long Sunday strolls was to be swept away, together with the parrot house, the pond and all diseased shrubs. A new bowling green would be laid out and the tennis courts converted into a children's playground. The idea of filling in the pond caused a public outcry and was later quietly dropped.

FEBRUARY.

11th   The City Hall was the venue for the first ever degree ceremony in the 22-year life of Hull's University College. It was a colourful occasion with processions of capped-and-gowned dignitaries in crimson, blue and yellow, together with scarlet-robed Mayors and Mayoresses, receiving a welcome from the President, Lord Middleton. Graduates were presented with their degrees by Professor Lillian Penson, the Vice Chancellor of London University.

15th   There was news of a proposed flying boat service linking Hull with Glasgow, Leith, Belfast, Southampton and Falmouth using 50-seater Hythe aircraft. Like so many aviation schemes of the time it was destined to remain 'just an idea'.

23rd   A bright sunny day encouraged a near record turnout for the General Election. The MPs elected were: Hull North - W.R. Austen Hudson (Conservative); Hull Central - Capt. Mark Hewitson (Labour); Hull East - Comdr. Harry Pursey (Labour); Hull Haltemprice - Richard Law (Conservative). North Hull had the highest poll at 86.3%. With the disappearance of the Hull North-West and Hull South-West divisions, Labour MPs R.W. Mackay and Alderman S.H. Smith had withdrawn from the campaign.

Sutton and Leads Road (Prefab) Tenants Association was formed to serve an estate of temporary homes 'out in the wilds' where an hourly bus service and the local pub were the only amenities. The 500 tenants, mostly young couples, decided to band together to run a Sunday school and gardening club, organise children's outings and campaign for better services.

Hull trawler engineers and firemen staged a 17 day strike over the share out of cod liver oil money, a small 'perk' that made all the difference to their incomes after a poor trip. At its peak 130 trawlers were tied up and only 30 of the fleet still at sea. St. Andrew's Dock was so congested that boats had to be moved to other docks and thousands of men were without work in an unusual conflict involving two sections of the same union - the Transport & General. The men returned to sea on 4th March.

MARCH.

21st   The Lord Mayor opened **Sidney Zimmerman Ltd.'s furniture shop** in Ferensway, opposite the Regal Cinema. In pre-opening advertising the 'palatial premises' (actually a temporary prefabricated building leased from the Corporation) boasted over £50,000 worth of stock - 'the largest stock of superior furniture seen in Hull for 15 years.'

21st   Hull became the first city in Britain to organise a drive for blood donors. The three-week campaign was advertised in shops and cinemas while at Paragon Station a 'Rhesus Baby Exhibit' was staged.

25th   Hull Register Office married no fewer than 38 couples, one every ten minutes. With couples qualifying for immediate tax rebates, it was the busiest day of the year for weddings. The four main churches had 30 weddings between them.

Restoration of the Alfred Gelder Street facade of the bomb-ravaged **Head Post Office** was nearing completion. Workmen had made an excellent job of matching the new stonework to the old but there was still a hole in the top storey to remind citizens of 'Hitler's visit'. Several of Hull's devastated central thoroughfares such as King Edward Street were looking bright and cheerful as a result of the Corporation's policy of planting bulbs and spring flowers. But five years after hostilities ceased there was still little evidence of re-construction.

Following complaints from residents near Sculcoates Power Station that they lived in perpetual 'rain' caused by condensation droplets from the 150 ft. wide cooling tower, Hull was chosen to experiment a project by London researchers to eliminate the nuisance by fitting a criss-crossed timber filter over the mouth of the tower.

APRIL.

3rd It was a sad night for regular devotees of Hull's oldest dance hall, the Fulford Hall on Beverley Road. Manager Freddie Roe staged the last public dance there before the place was sold. A popular venue for nearly 40 years, many of the patrons were the children of those who had met there a generation back. During the war, after being used to store furniture from bombed out homes and as NFS dormitories, the Fulford had entertained visiting sailors and seamen. Admission on the final night cost 3/-.

10th Several people were seasick on the Humber Ferry when a freak gale reached 70 mph. The 1.15 p.m. crossing had to be suspended.

13th At a ceremony in Queens Gardens, seven Japanese flowering cherry trees brought specially from Holland were planted near the Dock Offices as a token of friendship between Great Britain and the Netherlands. Dr. P.J. Oud, the Burgomaster of Rotterdam, paid tribute to Britain's armed services for helping to restore the liberty of the Dutch people.

24th The Lord Mayor laid the foundation stone for 24 flats in Pearson Park to be known as **Henson Villas**. They were to be reserved for single women in order to release family houses for re-letting.

A pleasant splash of green was created in the Old Town with the laying out of an attractive Georgian garden behind **Wilberforce House**. Featuring a lawn, fan-shaped ornamental trees and an arboured gateway to the River Hull, it was built on the site of the old-time street designed in the late-1930s by Mr. Tom Sheppard (Curator of Museums) but then sadly burnt out with the loss of all exhibits. The wrought iron entrance came from the old Trinity House Almshouses in Anlaby Road.

Work was going on by day and night in a big push to complete a gigantic grain silo at the Cleveland Street mill of **Spillers Ltd**. in time for the harvest. The £135,000 structure was designed to hold 10,000 tons of grain taken in from either lorries or craft on the River Hull. Standing on a foundation of 600 reinforced concrete piles, it was being built by a novel process - continuous concreting with the sliding shuttering jacked upwards every few minutes.

The building of 500 homes on the **Bricknell Avenue Estate** was nearing completion. Only 54 flats, six shops and a school were required to finish phase one. The estate was to be surrounded by an informal park or 'green belt'. A further 500 homes were envisaged on the nearby West Bulls Farm site once deep drainage reached the area by the early-1960s.

MAY.

5th After years of delay and frustration caused mainly by steel shortages and the economic climate, the Government finally gave the blitzed cities the go-ahead to make a limited start on large-scale reconstruction. In Hull any jubilation soon turned to disappointment when the Ministry announced the year's capital allocation for such works. Corporation officials were astonished that, after bidding for £1 million, the city was only allocated a meagre £50,000, half the amount allocated to Plymouth, Coventry and Portsmouth. The full cost of restoring the city centre was estimated at many millions but several projects were ready and waiting including Hammonds, the Cecil Cinema, the W.H. Smith's site in Jameson Street and 'Block 41A' in Ferensway. Later in May a deputation comprising Alderman Body, Alderman Spruit, the Town Clerk and Town Planning Officer met Dame Evelyn Sharp at the Ministry of Town & Country Planning to protest at Hull's treatment and obtained an assurance that more money would soon be on the way. Given the state of the economy, the serious shortage of materials and limited capacity of the building industry, the capital allocation system was used until 1953 to 'ration' development thus ensuring that only priority work was undertaken. It was left to the local authority to divide it up among individual schemes.

15th Wash day was thrown into chaos and many people had to go without a cooked mid-day meal when power cuts hit the Hull area after a plant breakdown at Sculcoates Power Station.

20th Councillor H. Fairbotham declared open a room at **Wilberforce House** that had been restored with Georgian pine panelling and beautiful floral wood carvings dating from the 1740s. The fittings were rescued from No. 21 High Street (a period house demolished after bomb damage) through the generosity of Mr. Philip Priestman in memory of his father William Dent Priestman, a man who was interested in Wilberforce's ideals.

The last of Hull Corporation's working horses, an 18 year old mare called Tidy, was retired from duty after a lifetime's service in East Park, pulling the grass cutter, moving rockery stones and helping with other heavy work. Horse-power had been gradually replaced by tractors and the faithful animals were either sold to humane

The Lord Mayor and civic party touring the newly-extended Covered Market when it opened in July 1950. The development made it possible to walk through to the original market hall from Lowgate. Photograph by courtesy of Hull City Record Office.

The Commonwealth Homes in Hartoft Road, a group of old people's bungalows, were built with the aid of a £30,000 grant from the National Air Raid Distress Fund, to which the Commonwealth countries had subscribed. Photograph by courtesy of Hull City Record Office.

owners or retired to paddocks at Sutton.

JUNE.

1st   The Alamein, the world's most modern trawler, went on trials on the Humber. Built for Hull Merchants Amalgamated Trawlers Ltd. the £100,000 oil burning ship was designed to speed her 28-man crew at over 13 knots to the furthest fishing grounds of Newfoundland and Greenland.   With full air-conditioning and central heating, her crew facilities were luxurious compared with existing boats. She could store 120 barrels of cod liver oil and her wireless transmitter was as large as the Queen Mary's.

5th   Sir George Wilkinson, a former Lord Mayor of London, opened the '**Commonwealth Homes**', 26 old people's bungalows on the Bricknell Avenue Estate. They were designed by the City Architect and erected for the Corporation by J. Mather & Son with a grant from the Lord Mayor of London's National Air Raid Distress Fund. Half the fund (to which Hull had contributed £26,000) came from the British Dominions and in tribute each house was named after an important Commonwealth city. The attractive brick buildings were grouped around a big central garden and there was a spacious communal hall for dining and lounging. Each home had a bedroom, living room, kitchenette, bathroom and all-electric central heating. Hull was only the third city to open such homes.

6th   A team of eleven local entertainers visited the BBC recording studios in Leeds to do battle for their city in Barney Colehan's popular Home Service radio quiz 'Top Town'. Taking part were: Norman Collier (farmyard impressions), Clarice McCunnell and Les Brooks, partnered by Harry Hemingway and his harmonica, Marion Campbell (crooner) and The Crackerjacks (Joan Richardson, Jean Best, Roy Longbottom and Peter Middleton). The Hull team emerged victorious in the heat against Cleethorpes and went on to beat Bury in the final broadcast on 29th June.

7th   Citizens flocked to Hull's coolest spot, the Pier, as temperatures climbed to 91 degrees in the shade.

10th After eight months of hard work converting the old Congregational Church in Hessle Road into a well equipped theatre, members of the Sizer-Simpson Repertory Company opened with a production of Maeterlinck's "The Blue Bird". Known later as the **Janus Theatre** and as a member of the Little Theatre Guild of Great Britain the resident Company, under the guidance of its professional

director Stella Sizer-Simpson, aimed to present in each season a widely ranged programme of six productions drawn from the works of major playwrights.

22nd Hull's many drama enthusiasts gained another new stage on which to practise their talents when the Sheriff inaugurated an **Open Air Theatre** in East Park. The parkland setting proved ideal for the first production - 'The Merry Wives of Windsor' by the Drasdo Repertory Company.

29th Hundreds of obsolete wartime gas masks were destroyed in a fire at Les Parker's Craven Street scrap yard.

It was announced that work would soon begin on a £1 million block scheme on the bombed site bounded by Waterworks Street, King Edward Street and Jameson Street.   To promote its speedy re-development the area had been bought up by the Corporation from 37 different owners and then leased to a London finance company, Ravenseft Properties Ltd. A high quality scheme of imposing neo-Georgian blocks 3 and 4-storeys high was envisaged by the architects, Donald Hamilton, Wakeford & Partners, helping to bring much-needed trade and activity back into the city centre. There were to be 50 shops, let mainly to bombed-out traders, and a car park in the centre. However the decision to lease the site to an 'out of town' firm soon caused a furore among the business community and prompted Hull's Chamber of Trade to table counter-proposals for a development led by the traders themselves.   Special Council meetings were called by the opposition Municipal Association Group (MAG) to try to get the decision reversed but without success.   The matter was only resolved after a deputation of interested parties met the Minister of Town & Country Planning who eventually agreed to the Ravenseft scheme, allowing work on the first phase to begin in November.

JULY.

4th   The Local Savings Committee heard that membership of savings groups had risen by 11,000 to over 56,000 in just two years. School savings group membership was up 24% and Hull topped a list of 14 large cities for average savings per person at 9s.1d. Similar news was a regular feature of the 'fifties, the city holding a proud record in the National Savings 'league table'.

14th The Corporation opened an extension to the **Covered Market** to accommodate some of the traders who had been blitzed out of the old Shambles. For hygiene reasons the 23 new stalls were restricted

A barren scene in Ferensway as Hammond's patiently await the go-ahead to reconstruct their department store. Building work was subject to licensing control to ensure scarce materials were used in the best national interest. Photograph by courtesy of Hull City Record Office.

Meanwhile, as far as possible it was 'business as usual' in these prefabricated buildings at the corner of Jameson Street and South Street. The Holderness Road (no. 64) trolleybus terminus was conveniently close by. Photograph by courtesy of Hull City Record Office.

With an extensive waterfront to protect, the fireboat 'Clara Stark' performed a vital role for the City of Hull Fire Brigade. She was usually moored in Humber Dock Basin, awaiting the call to action. Photograph by courtesy of Innes Studios, Hessle.

Councillor J.S. Wilson, Chairman of the West Hull and Haltemprice Main Drainage Scheme Joint Committee, driving the first trench pile to set the project in motion in May 1950. Photograph by courtesy of Hull City Record Office.

to selling butcher's meat and provisions and not allowed to trade in 'dusty root vegetables', a ruling which displeased some of the stallholders at first.

17th Train services had to be cancelled when signals and points failed near Paragon Station after a railway engine crashed into the wall at the back of Western General Hospital severing power cables.

Towering high above Drypool Bridge the steelwork was almost in place at Ranks' **Clarence Flour Mill**, a replacement for the mill destroyed by bombing that was once among the largest in Britain. By mid-1952 the new plant would be employing the latest technology to produce 90,000 tons of flour a year in the city where, 75 years before, the late Joseph Rank had single-handedly turned out two-dozen sacks of flour a week from his Holderness Road windmill.

AUGUST.

5th More than 30,000 people attended the biggest ever East Park Gala which began with a procession of decorated floats from Dansom Lane. The Gala Queen was installed and a children's fancy dress parade judged at the new open air theatre. Jointly organised by the Parks Department and Sailors Children's Society, a thrilling programme was lined up: Buck Ryan's cowboy rodeo, the Mercury Riders dare-devil motorcyclists, the Royal Troupe of Alsatians, the Donna Roma London Ballet, fire fighting demonstrations, water jet football, bicycle polo, baseball, netball, archery, gymnastics, a youth choir concert, pet show, model boating, a road safety competition and dancing. Even Hull's councillors joined in the fun - riding ponies in the 'Southcoates Stakes' gymkhana! The day was rounded off with a grand fireworks display.

Hull Fishing Vessel Owners Association decided to lay up a fifth of the trawler fleet tonnage because the industry was in depression. Fish landings were heavy but demand was the weakest some merchants had known in fifty years. With a wider choice of items for the table such as rabbits, eggs and a larger bacon ration, housewives seemed to be turning away from fish as a main meal.

SEPTEMBER.

2nd Over a thousand Polish refugees streamed down the gangway of the ss. *Dundalk Bay* in King George Dock, at the end of a trek of thousands of miles. They arrived from Mombasa where they had been sent by the British Government after being handed over by Russia when she entered the war. They were taken to the hostel for displaced persons in Priory Road to await allocation to farm duties or unskilled work.

5th The Lord Mayor opened the premises of **Brown Brothers Ltd.** (motor parts dealers), one of the first to be occupied in the new Reform Street/Francis Street factory estate. The area had been specially laid out by the Corporation for light industries and distributive traders that needed to be near the city centre. It marked the start of a Council plan to shift industry to designated zones away from inner-city housing so that residents were no longer disturbed by heavy goods traffic, noise, smells and grime. Other industrial estates were planned for Clough Road, Bankside, Chamberlain Road, Leeds Road, Stoneferry, English Street and Anlaby Road (the last to accommodate motor traders).

24th British Railways axed winter Sunday trains from Hull to Hornsea and Withernsea to save money. They claimed that it cost £83 to run trains on a typical Sunday but receipts averaged only £8.

25th At the Housing Committee Councillor Hurley demanded the rehousing of the residents of Cheapside and Provident Place without delay. He claimed they could see stars through the roof and said it was a scandal anyone had to live in such 'abominable dives'. The homes had been on the condemned list since 1927.

OCTOBER.

16th There was some excitement in the Anlaby Road area when a Rhesus monkey was spotted on the rooftops after escaping from Hull Fair. It was first seen by a fitter at the East Yorkshire bus depot and a crowd gathered to watch its antics as it defied capture. Later a sighting was made in Spring Bank Cemetery. After being hunted in vain by men with nets for several days, the cold and hungry animal was eventually put out of its misery in the National Avenue area by an expert RSPCA marksman. Householders had been afraid to open their windows while it was at large.

18th Automation was gradually coming to Hull's Fish Dock. An improved method of cleaning fish kits (the 10 stone tubs in which fish was packed for quayside sale) was adopted. Instead of scrubbing them by hand in cold water a battery of three automatic machines was installed, each capable of washing 5,000 kits per eight hour shift with less labour. The kits were subjected to jets of steam under pressure and then rinsed in hot and cold water. Aluminium kits were now starting to replace the wooden ones traditionally made by Sutherland & Tate's of Hawthorn Avenue.

21st   An event long-awaited by citizens who recalled its pre-war popularity was the reopening of **Jacksons Paragon Ballroom**. It had been completely rebuilt with an extra floor by Stepney Ltd. of Beverley and boasted a 250 seat ballroom, a restaurant for 180 diners and a small function room. The ballroom featured the latest automatic colour-change concealed lighting system.

26th   The Rev. W. Edwin Sangster (President of the Methodist Conference), well-known for his progressive preaching, was the guest of honour at Thornton Hall (St. George's) Methodist Mission's 73rd anniversary. It was the final service before the mission closed for war damage repairs.

The 630 home Garden Village Estate in East Hull, inaugurated in 1908 by Sir James Reckitt for his factory workers, was sold to the Bradford Property Trust Ltd. Since July tenants had been offered the chance to buy their own homes.

NOVEMBER.

16th   Another phase of **Trinity House Rest Homes** on Anlaby High Road near White City was opened by the Master Warden, Captain J.L.P. Sibree. The scheme, begun in 1940, was intended to replace several scattered almshouses at Kingston College, Posterngate and 'The Ship' - the blitzed mariners' homes in Carr Lane. By May 1951 32 new homes would be ready for aged seamen and their widows.

18th   Trolleybuses on the Holderness Road and Anlaby Road routes were halted by a power failure just as thousands of supporters were heading for Craven Park to see Rovers play Castleford and Boothferry Park for City's match against Q.P.R. The circuit was overloaded because too many buses were in the central section at once.

24th   Flood water gushed over doorsteps in the Chapman Street area before dawn when the Foredyke Stream overflowed its western bank after a tidal door collapsed near North Bridge. The floods recurred at each high tide for two days until workers from Beverley shipyard managed to fix a new steel door. Some residents had no light or gas and a terrible smell hung around their homes. A fifty-strong crowd of angry housewives stormed the Guildhall complaining about the lack of official relief.

DECEMBER.

5th   After building alterations Hull Jail was turned into a Borstal institution for hardened young offenders and the 30 inmates and their warders were transferred to other prisons.

18th   Hull's civic Christmas tree, a gift from the Norwegian town of Aalesund, was erected on a new site in Queens Gardens and the decorations were switched on by Synnore Liaaen, a student and native of that town. For the pantomime season Goons star Harry Secombe was appearing in 'Jack & The Beanstalk' at the New Theatre while at the Tivoli it was 'Mother Goose' with Charlie Ellis.

By the year end there were new signs of life in the city centre with construction workers beavering away on a number of sites: **Brook Chambers** (Ferensway/Brook Street); **W.H. Smith's** (Jameson Street); **Jordan & Co. (Hull) Ltd.** (Story Street); **Hammonds Ltd.** (Paragon Square); **Ravenseft Properties** (Waterworks Street/King Edward Street); **Edwin Davis & Co. Ltd.** (Bond Street); **Shell House** (Ferensway); **Seaton's Buildings** (Paragon Square). At last the rebuilding of Hull was under way.

LIVING CONDITIONS IN 1951.	
Hull's population in 1951	298,100
Total number of households in the city	94,800
Families sharing a dwelling	4,900
Households with no piped water supply	13,200
Dwellings with no fixed bath	34,000
Families with a shared bath	7,300
Dwellings with no kitchen sink	15,600
Families sharing a kitchen sink	7,000
Families sharing a cooker	6,200

Information from 1951 Census of Population.

Polish refugees coming ashore at King George Dock to begin a new life in Britain after their long voyage from Mombasa aboard the S.S. Dundalk Bay. Photograph by courtesy of Innes Studios, Hessle.

UNEMPLOYMENT - A TIME FOR ACTION!

Although unemployment was not crippling by today's standards the number of people looking for work in Hull remained stubbornly above the national average throughout the 'fifties. In 1950 for instance it averaged 3.5% of the working population compared with 1.5% for Great Britain as a whole.

By the autumn of that year, news that the jobless total had risen above 5,000 prompted a large group of men who were fed up with the constant fruitless search for work to hold an unofficial protest meeting at the Employment Exchange and send a deputation to see the Lord Mayor to plead for action.

They were mainly labourers and semi-skilled workers whose plight was brought about by the shortage of construction work. When men had been set on for the rebuilding of Hammonds and the Shell Mex building there had been twenty men chasing every job.

The Lord Mayor held out little immediate hope of absorbing the men unless the Government increased Hull's reconstruction programme. But he was sympathetic to their plight and invited Ministry of Labour officials and members of the Development and Employment Committees to the Guildhall for a special crisis conference to see what could be done. An immediate appeal was issued to Council departments and the large firms to do all they could to offer work. The help of the University College was also enlisted to make an exhaustive survey of the situation and the capabilities of the people on the register.

The problem was not one of industrial decline; quite the opposite for spectacular progress was being made with replacing the three million square feet of factory space lost in the war. Rather it reflected an ever increasing, insatiable demand for jobs by Hull's predominantly young population. The city desperately needed to attract new factory developments that would mop up the surplus labour by providing several hundred new vacancies at once. The Lord Mayor therefore agreed to write to the Board of Trade urging them to speed up the issue of licences to firms keen to expand here, one of which was known to be Montague Burton Ltd. who wanted to build a big clothing factory.

In mid-November three men - Dan Boyall, Bill Ward and Les Sutton - decided to hitch hike to London to put the case of Hull's workless 5,000 before the Employment Minister (Mr. George Isaacs). They felt that their personal suffering best placed them to present the problem effectively to the 'powers that be'. Dan Boyall carried a battered case containing documents answering every point Mr. Isaacs was likely to make. After spending a miserable night 'kipped down' in the waiting room at Kings Cross they met the four local MPs and Mr. Arthur Moody, a Hull-born MP to whom they had been introduced by Mr. Robert Tarran (a well-known businessman who supported their cause) to go over their arguments. The weary trio spent two days in the capital before returning to Hull by train using tickets the MPs had bought for them.

Although some of their work-creating ideas could not be adopted at a time of numerous controls and restrictions, they did achieve some success. Hull's Housing Committee agreed to create a number of unskilled jobs by ordering 100 mass-produced prefab-type Corporation houses and the city's MPs persuaded the Government to allow an early start on two major drainage schemes requiring 470 men.

As the decade moved on the picture brightened for a time as reconstruction work got into full swing, several local firms managed to secure some prestigious orders and new employers like Imperial Typewriters made their home in Hull. By 1956 the unemployment rate had in fact dwindled to 1.8%. However there was little time to sit back and rejoice. By the winter of 1958/9 the position had become worse than ever, with 6,250 or 4.6% of the workforce seeking jobs. As a result, and following sustained pressure from local interests, the Board of Trade agreed to include Hull in their list of places eligible for special grant aid and assistance to industry.

With unemployment at an unacceptable peak in late 1950, Dan Boyall, Bill Ward and Les Sutton hitch-hiked to London to plead with the Government Minister for action to create jobs in Hull. Photograph by courtesy of Innes Studios, Hessle.

The gloomy job situation brightened for a time when Imperial Typewriters opened a new factory in Hull. Here a group of businessmen see for themselves how typewriters are made. Photograph by courtesy of Innes Studios, Hessle.

On 1st May, 1951, civic leaders watch as the Lord Mayor (Councillor H.J. Barney) lays the foundation stone for Festival House in Jameson Street, the first permanent city centre building to be erected in post-war Hull. Photograph by courtesy of Hull City Record Office.

1951

The year that:-

His Majesty the King opened the Festival of Britain from the steps of St. Paul's.

Aneurin Bevan, John Freeman and Harold Wilson resigned from the Government over the introduction of charges for dental care and spectacles.

The Conservatives won the General Election and Winston Churchill once again became Prime Minister.

The Archers, Ambridge's 'country folk', began their long-running radio serial.

Foreign Office diplomats Maclean and Burgess defected to the Russians.

JANUARY.

3rd The first youth was ordered to attend Hull's new **Juvenile Attendance Centre**, one of only three to be set up in Britain after the Children's Committee agreed to co-operate in a Home Office experiment. For stealing a penknife from a shop, the 13 year old had to give up twelve consecutive Saturday mornings to attend lectures, handicrafts and P.T. sessions at the centre.

6th Football history was made in Hull when B1-type steam locomotive No. 61080, decorated with a large blue and yellow rosette, pulled an eight coach train with 600 supporters aboard into the new **Boothferry Park Halt** - the first train ever to serve a football club at its own gate. Nearly 5,000 fans travelled from Paragon Station via the overhead goods line to see City's Cup tie against Everton for a 6d. return fare. The new service was designed to speed crowd movement and ease congestion on the roads.

9th Thos. Hamlings' trawler *St. Leander* (H.19) was lost after colliding in the Humber. All the crew were rescued but the wreck had to be blown up when a salvage attempt failed.

15th As part of a desperate national drive to save coal, the Railway Executive cancelled 36 daily train services operating to or from Paragon Station.

Hull's last petrol-engined bus, RH 4758, began a new life as a mobile theatre. After being fitted out with a fold-up stage and dressing rooms at the Corporation Transport workshops, the green and cream vehicle was set to spend the next 25 summers touring the housing estates bringing entertainment to children who lived some distance from the parks. Punch & Judy shows, marionettes, concerts and dance band performances were some of the treats lined up.

FEBRUARY.

1st Three hundred 'children of all ages' enjoyed an express rail excursion to Nottingham to see 'Red Riding Hood' at the Theatre Royal, with lunch and tea served on the train. Pantomime trips such as this one organised by the Hull Daily Mail are a well remembered feature of life in the 'fifties.

27th A grand occasion for lovers of good music was provided by the reopening of the **City Hall organ** following a £20,000 restoration. The organ was built by local experts Messrs. Forster & Andrews in 1911 but completely ruined in the wartime conflagration of May 1941. With the benefit of advice from Holy Trinity organist Mr. Norman Strafford, it had been fully restored and the tonal scheme enlarged. Councillor H. Fairbotham described it as the finest instrument of its kind in existence. After Mr. J. Taylor of the John Compton Organ Co. had described its special features, recitals were given by Fernando Germani and Norman Strafford.

MARCH.

5th Hull's locally-owned New Theatre was sold to a West End company, the Whitehall Theatre Ltd., for £78,000. Under the shrewd management of Peppino Santangelo, the 'New' had grown from modest roots in the Little Theatre next door into a large, complex body with a theatrical reputation second to none. Though financially sound it needed extra capital to develop. Its new owners pledged to bring the best touring companies to the city.

6th The paddle steamer *Lincoln Castle* was badly damaged in a mid-Humber collision with her sister ship, the *Tattershall Castle*, in thick fog. After a terrific bump passengers were flung on to the decks and windows and crockery were broken.

16th Eleven local people lost their lives in one of the worst rail accidents of modern times when the 8.45 a.m. train from Hull (combined with the 9.15 a.m. from York to form the 10.06 a.m. 'Cock of the North' express to London Kings Cross) crashed at Balby Bridge Junction just outside Doncaster Station. Witnesses reported a tearing and splintering of wood as the carriages telescoped and crashed into the base of a tunnel. Two of the coaches were derailed and lay broadside across the track blocking all the main lines. Railway staff hurried to the scene and, after some dramatic rescue efforts, the casualties were rushed by ambulances to Doncaster Infirmary. The final death toll was 14 - eight men, five women and a baby. It was 10 p.m. the next day before the main down route was reopened.

22nd Leeds Regional Hospital Board set up a mass radiography unit offering free chest X-rays at the former Hull & Sculcoates Dispensary in Baker Street. Corporation employees, teachers, nurses and hospital staff were among the first to be examined. A mobile unit also toured the district, visiting the University and major industrial firms, in a big campaign to defeat the killer disease tuberculosis by the early detection of chest abnormalities.

APRIL.

13th Hull construction firm Spooners Ltd. secured a £3.6 million order from Australia for 2,000 prefabricated timber bungalows to be delivered over a two year period. A delighted Mr. J.L. Spooner cabled the news home while flying from Australia to America, promising 200 new jobs to help relieve the serious unemployment situation.

14th Hull Corporation Transport introduced City Bus Tours on Summer Sundays and Bank Holidays. There were three one-hour trips to choose from, taking in housing and social developments, industries and the docks. The tours immediately proved very popular as both cars and petrol were in short supply and citizens were anxious to observe the post-war rebuilding and growth of their city. They were repeated each year up to 1954.

27th Lord Crook (Chairman of the National Dock Labour Board) opened a new club for Hull dockers at **The Willows, Holderness Road**. Described as the largest and finest dockers club in the country, it had several meeting rooms, a concert hall, billiards room and three acres of grounds for tennis, bowls and fishing.

30th West Hull and Haltemprice were among the areas worst affected by 25% 'load-shedding' power cuts when an unseasonable cold snap struck while generators were out of action. Homes and factories were without power for over three hours from 8 a.m.

The Lord Mayor described as 'wonderful news for the unemployed' the announcement that an immediate start was to be made on a new £500,000 factory for the Leicester-based Imperial Typewriter Company on a 14 acre site on Hedon Road. With plans to build up the labour force to 3,000 ultimately (ambitious hopes which were never actually realised), it was the biggest new factory project for many years. Half the production would go for export. The move to Hull came because Leicester had full employment and no spare labour to allow expansion.

The Allotments Sub-Committee resolved to allow no more pigsties to be set up on Hull allotments. Pig keeping and 'pig clubs' (where tenants banded together to buy and fatten animals) had been very popular in days of food shortage but now interest was dwindling. During hot, dry weather the smells emanating from the sties brought numerous complaints, especially where they were close to houses.

MAY.

1st A momentous event took place in Jameson Street when the Lord Mayor and Alderman W. Body (Chairman of the Town Planning Committee) laid foundation stones on the site of **Festival House** to commemorate the first permanent structure to be built in the city centre since the 1941 blitz. During the ceremony fanfares were sounded by buglers of No.6 (Boys) Training Regiment Royal Corps of Signals and flags flown from the Guildhall and City Hall. Mementoes such as coins and stamps, a booklet on the city, a copy of the day's Hull Daily Mail and a Festival of Britain programme were placed in cavities under the stones. This pioneering development of shops and offices was, appropriately, owned by the Corporation on behalf of the people of Hull. Design work was by C. Cowles Voysey and J. Brandon Jones and the main contractors were Leslie & Co. Ltd.

4th Councillor Mrs T. Shepperdson opened Hull's second **Corporation Day Nursery** at St. Mungo House, 449 Holderness Road. She explained that nurseries like this and the one at Pearson Park supported the country's economy at a time when more and more women were having to go out to work. A charge of 1/- a day was made for the service.

19th Hull's Festival of Britain exhibition opened (*see page 29*).

Hull 1950s Entertainers

RONNIE HILTON, born in Gipsyville. Attended Francis Askew, Paisley Street and Ainthorpe Schools. After singing in the clubs, began recording, broadcasting and TV work in 1954, his second record 'I Still Believe' / 'Veni, Vedi, Vici' becoming a hit and bringing instant fame. His version of 'No Other Love' topped the charts for 6 weeks in 1956. Starred in summer shows and pantos all over Britain.

LEFT : Sir BRIAN RIX, born at Cottingham, the son of a Hull shipowner. Began a 30 year run as an actor/manager in 1950, presenting and appearing in stage productions, films and TV farces. His best known 'Whitehall Farces' included Reluctant Heroes (1950-4), Dry Rot (1954-8) and Simple Spyman (1958-61). Gained recognition for his work for people with mental handicap and knighted by Her Majesty The Queen in 1986. Chairman of MENCAP.

IAN CARMICHAEL, trained at Sandhurst and served in Europe with the 22nd Dragoons. Endeared himself to millions of fans throughout the 1950s in West End theatre, radio, TV and films. A notable performance was in Lucky Jim in 1957.

LEFT : NORMAN COLLIER, a building trade worker, developed his natural talent for comedy the hard way through the Northern clubs, turning professional in 1952 at the Tivoli Theatre. Went on to make his name in cabaret and seaside variety shows, also in numerous pantomimes where his outrageously funny Dame often stole the show.

21st   Sixteen elderly men were taken by bus from Beverley Road Hostel to begin a new life in an elegant country house at Sutton. **Dunbar House**, the new name for Sutton Grange following its renovation from a derelict shell, was the first of four 'Kingston Homes' opened in 1951 by the Welfare Services Department in pursuit of their policy of phasing out the old ex-workhouse hostels. In the new homes there were no rules and regulations, residents were free to come and go as they liked, and weekly cinema shows and outings were planned. The other converted homes were at **North Ferriby** (Manor House), **Pearson Park** and **Hessle** (Mentone House). Five purpose-built homes were also envisaged as soon as building restrictions eased.

A unique book telling of the self-sacrifice, heroism and steadfastness of Hull civilians who volunteered for rescue and welfare work during the 1939-45 war was published by the Corporation. 'A North East Coast Town' by Tom Geraghty (former assistant editor of the Hull Daily Mail) had been intended for private circulation but by public demand over 3,000 copies were put on sale at the Civil Defence headquarters in Queens Gardens for 5/- each.

JUNE.

11th   Ferensway was thronging with people and traffic when 54 buses set off for Scarborough taking 1,800 Hull Co-operative Society employees and their families on their annual excursion. It was thought to be the biggest fleet ever to leave Hull.

20th-30th   The Festival of Britain ship, HMS *Campania*, was in port (*see page 31*).

26th   Hull's **Development Plan**, a document prepared by the Council under town and country planning legislation to guide the city's development for the next twenty years, was delivered to the Ministry of Local Government and Planning by Corporation officials. It was the only one in the area ready in time to meet the Ministry's 30th June deadline. The plan was on a more practical scale than the earlier one produced by Sir Patrick Abercrombie on a wave of unbridled late-war optimism. The plan set out to provide for an estimated 1971 population of 304,000 and the cost of fulfilling it was put at £131 millions. Briefly it envisaged:
- building 24,000 new homes in 23 neighbourhood units each free from through traffic (including some outside the city boundary),
- concentrating industry in three belts along the Rivers Hull and Humber,
- reserving land for 23 primary and 30 secondary schools and colleges,
- eliminating five level crossings and three branch railway lines,
- a new Drypool Bridge and several major roads and car parks,
- fresh parks, playgrounds and open spaces (including a Town Park near the Pier) and
- a new dock beside the River Hull at Stoneferry.

A Public Inquiry to examine the plan, which opened on 6th November, was one of the largest seen at the Guildhall for many years. The Council Chamber was crowded with legal experts; huge maps were set up on the walls illustrating land use, population density, the age of buildings and so on, while in the foyer a massive relief model showed how Hull might look two decades on. Although 104 formal objections were lodged they were primarily concerned with how the plan affected certain property rather than critical of its concept.

A special Corporation sub-committee was set up to report on a matter of great public anxiety - Hull's unprotected open drains. Since 1940 13 children had been drowned, seven in the Barmston Drain alone, a favourite play haunt. About 25 miles of major agricultural drains crossed the city but according to legal opinion the Council was under no obligation to fence them. Later in the decade, when the Northern trunk sewer was completed, it became possible to fill-in three of the drains.

New boundary signs were being erected on the main approach roads. Featuring a shield bearing the three crowns of Hull hanging inside an oak frame, they were designed by Mr. W. Morris (City Engineer), an accomplished wood carver and painter. Poised above the shield was an impression of an early schooner cut in metal and presented to the city by Mr. Harold Sheardown of C.D. Holmes Ltd.

JULY.

11th   A dream of making Hull one of the premier provincial air centres in Britain ended with the disbanding of the Corporation's Aerodrome Committee. Located near Hedon, it had been the first municipal aerodrome in the country when opened by Prince George (later the Duke of Kent) in October 1929. Enthusiasm had run high at first: A Hull Aero Club had been formed, there had been talk of developing a seaplane base on the Humber and the Dutch airline KLM had made it a stopping place on its Amsterdam to Liverpool route. However the 230 acre site proved incapable of expansion to take the next generation of airliners. All efforts to get Hull and East Riding people to be 'air minded' and to use its facilities failed.

The city centre with a 'half built' appearance in 1951. Work was well advanced on the corner block of Queens House but much of King Edward Street (right) and Paragon Street had yet to start. Even so, there were plenty of people about and always a trolleybus to take them home. Photograph by courtesy of the Yorkshire Post.

East Ella Hall, a 15-bedroom mansion once owned by Robert Jameson (whose name was given to a city centre thoroughfare), had been the centrepiece of Hull's White City Pleasure Grounds. In 1951, with the cost of restoration prohibitive, it faced demolition. Photograph by courtesy of Hull City Record Office.

25

Raich Carter, Hull City's legendary player-manager from 1948 to 1951. Photograph by courtesy of Innes Studios, Hessle.

Hull Fair in full swing in October, 1951 after a dispute between the Corporation and the Showmen's Guild had been settled amicably. On the left can be seen the 'High Fliers' or steam yachts which Hull folk are in the habit of referring to as the 'Shamrock'. Photograph by courtesy of Hull City Record Office.

During the war the aerodrome became a rocket gun site and afterwards a speedway track. Most of the huts were sold off but the clubhouse was moved to Sutton Park Golf Club where it was opened in its new role by the Lord Mayor on 2nd July.

13th   The city centre was enveloped in a massive cloud of black smoke when a spectacular fire wrecked a large shed on Humber Dock causing around £100,000 worth of damage. Sixty firemen were busy at the height of the blaze which destroyed merchandise awaiting shipment including lollipop sticks, newsprint, tinned strawberries, oil drums and suit linings. People were driven back by the furnace-like temperatures even 20 yards away. Thanks to her quick acting crew the ss. *Melrose Abbey*, which was moored nearby, was swung into the centre of the dock out of danger. The cause was thought to be either a discarded cigarette or a gas leak.

A human skeleton was unearthed during the demolition of **Salem Chapel** in Cogan Street. The chapel, dating from 1833, had once been a Jewish Synagogue.

Work was well under way on a new East Stand at **Boothferry Park** in readiness for the opening of the football season.

Hull's population at the 1951 census was 299,068, showing a fall of 14,500 over twenty years. Most of the loss had been taken up by Haltemprice as people had moved out to the newer western suburbs. Hull was still the ninth largest city in England and Wales.

The first stage of **Priestman Brothers Ltd.'s** new £500,000 works at Marfleet had gone into production and foundations were being laid for stage two. The seven year project would see the entire works in Thomas Street relocated to the new site which was expected to employ 1,000. Priestman's manufactured grabs, excavators and dredging equipment and had a full order book for four years ahead.

AUGUST.

10th   Another sign of Hull's post-war industrial rebirth came when Mrs Arnold Reckitt, wife of the chairman of Reckitt & Sons Ltd., opened a new four-storey factory block at the firm's **Kingston Works** in the presence of civic guests and 2,000 employees and pensioners. Situated where Mr. Isaac Reckitt's original starch works had been a century earlier, it was the largest block on the Dansom Lane site and rose from the ruins of a blitzed laboratory and packing room for 'Reckitts Blue', one of the many household brand names for which the Hull firm was world famous.

The port of Hull was going through a period of exceptional activity. There was such a shortage of berths that ships laden with Cuban sugar, Finnish timber, American barley and many other commodities were having to queue in the river until dock spaces became free. One reason was that the Baltic timber season was at its peak and every available timber berth was occupied. Hull was now the nation's second port for importing softwood and trade was heading for a 12-15 year record. Vast quantities of grain were pouring in mainly from America, Canada and Australia and the King George Dock silo was working to capacity. Discharge was hampered by a shortage of dock workers and the National Dock Labour Board was having to recruit men from the ports of Goole, Grimsby and Southampton.

Three severe fires kept Hull Fire Brigade active during the month. Much of the roof collapsed in an afternoon blaze at Somerset Street Boys Senior School on 23rd.   Two days later the fireboat *Clara Stark* was rushed into service to fight a blaze among 1,000 tons of palm kernels at Waterloo Cake Mills, Cleveland Street watched by many sightseers. Then early on 27th £1,000 worth of damage was caused to the games room of the Adelaide Club in Staniforth Place.

Park keepers were reported to be 'at their wits end' with the amount of vandalism being done in the city's parks. At Pearson Park trees had been disfigured, flowers and shrubs trampled on, seats thrown into the pond, sticks cut to make bows and arrows and turf removed to find worms for tiddlering. Glass had been broken at Tower Grange nurseries. Two types of offender were noticed - very young children behaving thoughtlessly and teenagers roaming about in gangs trying to impress their girlfriends.

Hull's coal situation had become so serious that households faced their bleakest winter ever, with supplies likely to be cut to 22 cwt. per customer. Local MPs protested to the Minister of Fuel.

To the regret of many, advertisements started appearing on the sides of Hull Corporation's smart blue and white buses for the first time. The Transport Committee reluctantly decided to accept them to bring in extra revenue but only after a lively debate about what might be suitable. Some councillors thought religious and political themes should be taboo while one was against advertising alcoholic drinks.

SEPTEMBER.

12th It was announced after a board meeting that Raich Carter, the player-manager who had contributed so much to Hull City's recent fortunes, had resigned 'because of disagreement over the conduct of the club's affairs'. News of the resignation came as a shock both to the city and the football world. One of the finest inside forwards the game had ever produced, Carter had come from Derby in 1948, taking over the management role when Major Frank Buckley left for Elland Road. In his quest for success he brought such quality players to Boothferry Park as Alf Ackerman, Syd Gerrie, Viggo Jensen (the Great Dane), Don Revie and Neil Franklin. He had led the Tigers to promotion and set up many new records. Now without his inspiration the club, which only the previous year had been on the verge of First Division football, slipped down the league table until he could be persuaded to return and complete the playing side of his contract.

23th Former-Alderman Archibald Stark, a colourful Hessle Road character, died. A Council member since 1919, it was largely through his special interest in the fire service that the splendid East Hull fire station was built. As Honorary Commandant of Hull Auxiliary Fire Service he had assisted at many big air raid fires. His coffin was borne to Hedon Road Crematorium on a modern fire engine with 70 volunteer firemen parading behind.

The great New York fight between Randolph Turpin and Sugar Ray Robinson was featured for a week at the Dorchester and Criterion cinemas. Patrons were tempted in by advertisements declaring 'Sensational decision by referee in 10th round - was he right in awarding the fight to Robinson? Turpin says No! Come and see for yourself.'

Hull fishermen struck a new fishing ground south of Cape Farewell off the Greenland coast. Greenland fishing had previously been concentrated on the northern coast but the new ground, being 300 miles nearer home, allowed trawlers to complete a round trip in 19 days, helped by the recent innovation of radar to keep track of ice floes in fog or darkness. Merchants were pleased with the quality of fish brought back especially the large halibut catches.

OCTOBER.

1st The Education Committee heard that a programme to give all Hull schools electric lighting was nearing completion. Twenty-five schools had been converted from gas in the past two years, St.

George's Road being one of the last. Plans were also announced to re-house **Hull Grammar School** in new premises originally intended for a Secondary Modern School off Bricknell Avenue. Pupils and staff had been working in cramped conditions at the Leicester Street building for many years.

11th Hull Fair opened as usual at noon after a dispute, in which over 200 members of the Showmen's Guild had threatened to boycott the 653 year old event, was settled amicably. Anxious to improve the ancient fair, the Corporation had allocated two sites on the Walton Street ground normally occupied by long-standing tenants to newcomers. One of those displaced was the Wall of Death, a horizontal motorcycle ride which many regarded as highly dangerous. The decision led to a protracted row which at one point reached deadlock with neither side willing to negotiate. When the fair eventually went ahead it was the biggest ever, with 250 exhibitors packed into the 13½ acre ground, renewing the eternal argument as to which fair was largest - Hull, Newcastle or Nottingham. Several new rides made their debut: W. Noble's 'Rotor'; J. Collins 'Rolator' and 'Boomerang'; J. Farrar's 'Dodgem, Swirl and Cresta Run' and a novelty 'Bingo Game' (the rage of Battersea Park!) brought by Corrigans of Scarborough. They joined such old favourites as Sir Robert Fossett's Circus; the Dive Bomber; Shaw's Moonrocket; Green's Caterpillar; the Colorado Wild West Show; the Great Indian Torture; Tom Thumb (the world's smallest man); the 'Shamrock' steam yachts; galloping horses and, of course, Chicken Joe. Most sideshows were charging 6d. or 3d. a go but despite lower prices than before it turned out to be the poorest fair for crowds since the war.

12th The 'wonder of the modern age' - television - was brought fully to the people of Hull and East Riding when the new Holme Moss transmitter, situated high on the Pennines, opened in the evening. Sylvia Peters introduced the first programme which featured a ceremony at Manchester Town Hall to launch the service. 'Stars' who made their appearance during the inaugural week included Richard Dimbleby, Muffin the Mule, Richard Hearne (Mr. Pastry), Terry Thomas and Wilfrid Pickles. Despite all the pre-opening publicity, local dealers such as Sydney Scarborough, Comet and the Co-op reported no great rush to acquire receivers at first and test signals had proved variable especially in the central areas. One problem was interference from the ignition systems of passing vehicles. By the 15th 1,700 licences had been issued in Hull and two days later the Hull Daily Mail began listing programmes.

17th   Football fans, still feeling the loss of Raich Carter, were dismayed to learn that Don Revie (Tigers' £20,000 inside-right from Leicester) had asked for a transfer. He had a keen desire to get into the top grade of soccer by joining a First Division club. City reluctantly agreed to release him to Manchester City in exchange for £13,000 plus full-back Ernie Phillips.

20th   Councillor A.E. Wheelband, chairman of the Local Committee of the British Legion, handed over the keys to the first of 18 houses erected in Hotham Road by the **Douglas Haig Memorial Homes** scheme. To cater for disabled ex-service people they were specially designed with extra-wide stairs, landings and doors. Rents were fixed according to income with none exceeding 10/- a week plus rates.

25th   There were no surprises in the General Election, all four Hull MPs being returned to Westminster. North Hull, being the most marginal seat, was the focal point of the campaign. The Socialists held an eve of poll torchlight procession around North Hull Housing Estate, a thrilling spectacle that delighted the local children. For the first time in many years the count was staged at the City Hall.

NOVEMBER.

5th   To eliminate the dangers of 'Guy Fawkes Night' street bonfires, the Corporation decided to designate 24 official bonfire sites around the city. It was also agreed to spend £20 on supervised fireworks displays in each of the parks. Hull was believed to be the only place in the country to do this.

12th   After over 12 years of closure the curtain went up once again at Anlaby Road's **Palace Theatre**, a favourite night spot for Hull folk. Previously part of the Moss Empires theatre chain, the Palace had been bought by a local company headed by manager Harold Clarke. It had been re-seated, re-carpeted and given modern decor and new lighting throughout. The opening was performed by Gertie Gitana, famous variety star of the day, and the capacity audience included the Sheriff and his Lady. Billy Cotton and his Band headed the programme along with singers Alan Breeze and Doreen Stevens, the prices ranging from 1/6d. on the balcony to 21/- for a private box. Frank Matcham & Co. (the London architects who designed the theatre) were responsible for the renovations, the main contractors being Brown Builders (Hull) Ltd. Curtains and carpets were supplied by H. Goldstone & Sons and seating by Norris of Bond Street.

DECEMBER.

7th   Alderman J. Dunbar, chairman of the Welfare Services Committee, laid the foundation stone of **Hugh Webster House** in St. Luke's Street, the first of five purpose-built homes for the elderly in Hull. Veteran Socialist campaigner Dr. Hugh Webster watched the ceremony from his car.

10th   Hull's progressive public library service took another step forward when Mr. L.R. McColvin (Chief Librarian of Westminster and President-elect of the Library Association) opened two new sections at the Albion Street building, the **Commercial & Technical Library** and the **Music Library**. The latter included a collection of 1,000 gramophone records which immediately proved popular, 1,270 loans being made in the first eight days.

Hull Corporation were promoting a Kingston upon Hull Bill in Parliament. The main purpose was to seek powers to build a new Drypool Bridge but the opportunity was taken to include measures to amalgamate certain parishes, control bathing in open drains, provide robes for councillors and retain Hull's age-old tradition of ten stone coal bags (eight stone bags were usual elsewhere) among other items. However, at a Town Meeting held to discuss the bill, a clause empowering the Corporation to declare smokeless zones was defeated after property owners objected to the extra expense of buying new grates.

CITY & COUNTY OF KINGSTON UPON HULL

Festival of Britain

1951

The Chairman (Alderman Frederick Holmes)
and Members of the Development Committee
request the pleasure of your company at the

Opening of the Festival Exhibition

by A. J. CHAMPION, Esq., M.P.
(Parliamentary Secretary, Ministry of Agriculture and Fisheries)

at the City Hall, Kingston upon Hull
on Saturday, 19th May, 1951, at 2 p.m.

◆   ◆   ◆

Seats will be available on the Balcony until 1-50 p.m.

Please present this card at the Waterworks Street Entrance, City Hall, if arriving before 2 p.m.

Members of the Sizer-Simpson Repertory Company performing a scene from Christopher Fry's play "The Lady's not for Burning" at their Hessle Road theatre in December, 1951. Photograph by courtesy of Stella Sizer-Simpson.

The North-East Section of the Veteran Car Club of Great Britain organised a 36 mile rally around the Hull area to commemorate the Festival of Britain. Some of the cars and their owners travelled over on the Humber Ferry from an earlier rally in Grimsby. Photograph by courtesy of Innes Studios, Hessle.

THE FESTIVAL OF BRITAIN.

1951 was Festival of Britain year when Britain and everything British went on show to the world in a grand display of national pride and confidence in the future.

From the outset the City Council were anxious that Hull, as a major city, played a full part in the celebrations and during 1950 set up a Festival Sub-Committee chaired by Alderman Frederick Holmes to organise a programme of local events in conjunction with Hull's many commercial and cultural bodies.

One of the first steps was to plan a huge exhibition on the theme 'Country Comes to Town' on the 26 acre open space on Bricknell Avenue now occupied by Kelvin High School. This would have been the largest exhibition of its kind ever staged in the North of England. Hull's business firms were invited to make the event their 'shop window' while the agricultural side was entrusted to the East Riding Branch of the National Farmers Union.

In January the whole of Hull was cheered by the news that the King and Queen were planning to pass through the city in June on their way back from a Festival tour to Scotland. Their last visit, in August 1941, to view the aftermath of the blitz and their ready sympathy in Hull's darkest hour had endeared them to the citizens and the occasion was eagerly awaited.

The sub-committee put together a very full programme lasting from April to November but unfortunately not everything went entirely to plan. The waterlogged state of the showground and economic restraints imposed by re-armament caused the outdoor exhibition to be cancelled at short notice. Then there was disappointment that the Covent Garden Opera Company would not be making a planned visit. Later came sadness as the Royal tour was called off owing to His Majesty's poor state of health.

However the remaining programme contained something to please just about everybody including:
- a presentation of T.S. Eliot's 'Murder in the Cathdderal' in Holy Trinity Church sponsored by the Citizens Arts League,
- a veteran car parade,
- an exhibition of historic silverware made by Hull goldsmiths,
- a Festival Sports and Athletic Meeting at Malet Lambert School,
- a concert by the Yorkshire Symphony Orchestra at the City Hall,
- open days at the fire stations and waterworks,
- a shop window dressing competition run by the Chamber of Trade.

In place of the outdoor exhibition a more modest affair was substituted based on the City Hall. It ran from 19th to 26th May and was opened by Mr. A.J. Champion MP, Parliamentary Secretary to the Minister of Agriculture and Fisheries, whose arrival was a colourful spectacle with troups of the Household Cavalry, Coldstream Guards and King's Troup Royal Horse Artillery lined up in full ceremonial dress outside. For 1/- entrance fee visitors could see many of the products of Hull factories, hear music by the Black Dyke Mills Band and follow 'the Story of Wool', recalling the role of this commodity in making Hull Britain's third port way back in the 13th century. There were daily sheep shearing demonstrations and mannequin parades featuring wool products. A giant telephone sixteen times normal size, the idea of the Telephones Manager, made a powerful centrepiece.

Two hours after dawn on 18th June crowds lined the Humber foreshore to welcome the Festival of Britain ship, HMS *Campania*, to King George Dock. Senior Humber Pilot George Berry and four tugs expertly guided the 16,000 ton ex-aircraft carrier through the lockpits without a scratch and the staging of a ten day floating exhibition, the biggest ever produced, got under way. The display - set out on the flight deck and in a 300 ft. long hangar - was a miniature version of the South Bank show in London and included a radar view of the port of Hull and models of London airport, an underground railway and a jet engine. The route from the city centre was gaily decorated with bunting and flowers and big crowds including 2,000 schoolchildren a day flocked to the ship in cars and special coaches from all over the North. A total of 87,834 people visited the vessel before she headed south for Plymouth to continue her round Britain Festival tour.

A series of factory visits, an idea suggested by the Junior Chamber of Commerce, enabled Hull people to see their own industries at work. Parties of 20-50 people toured Reckitts, Waddingtons, Smith & Nephews, Premier Soap Co., the Y.E.B., Moors & Robsons, Hull Brewery, British Cod Liver Oil Products, B.O.C.M. and the Hull Daily Mail. The spring visits proved so popular that more had to be arranged in September.

Hull city centre in September, 1952. Some new buildings are in evidence such as Hammonds store (centre) and Jordans cycle dealers (top right) but there are many gaps waiting to be filled, especially along Prospect Street and Carr Lane. Reproduced from an original by Photoflight Ltd.

1952

The year that:-

King George VI died at Sandringham aged 56.

Identity cards were abolished.

A small Devon village was devastated when the River Lyn suddenly changed its course.

Gen. Eisenhower won a sweeping victory in the American Presidential election.

The last of the great 'pea-souper' smogs descended over London claiming at least 4,000 victims.

Agatha Christie's play 'The Mousetrap' began its eternal West End run.

The first cheap air flights were introduced.

JANUARY.

3rd   A flag flew at half mast over Clarence Mill after the death in London of millionaire miller and racehorse owner Mr. James Voase Rank. The Hull-born Chairman and managing director of J. Rank Ltd. was a past pupil of Courtney Street and Hymers Schools and elder brother of film magnate J. Arthur Rank. Only last October he had been in Hull to view reconstruction work on his Drypool flour mill.

12th   2,500 excited fans travelled to Old Trafford to see next-to-bottom Division Two club Hull City play First Division leaders Manchester United in a third round cup tie. To their surprise and delight the underdogs won 2-0 and United manager Matt Busby congratulated City's players on a fine showing. The Tigers were later knocked out by Blackburn Rovers.

24th   The Lord Mayor telephoned Mr. Harold Carr of Faversham Avenue from an exhibition at St. Martin's Church Hall and congratulated him on becoming the Corporation's 40,000th subscriber after a seven year wait for a phone. The call marked the opening of the nearby **West Hull Telephone Exchange**, a £150,000 development serving 3,800 users initially but capable of expanding to 6,000 to ease the waiting list in the Anlaby Park area.

30th   There was a spate of road accidents when freak fog and icy roads combined to make travel treacherous in the Hull area. A bus collided with an alcohol tanker on Anlaby High Road and five vehicles crashed near North Bridge when a shooting brake caught fire and a car ran away driverless.

30th   Animal movements were restricted in Hull and 44 cattle had to be slaughtered after Foot and Mouth disease was confirmed at Haverflatts Farm near County Road, the 22nd case since the disease hit the East Riding last November. Hull Cattle Market had been closed for three weeks.

One of the most up to date milk processing plants in East Yorkshire was brought into operation in Charles Street by **Clover Dairies Ltd**. It was designed by Messrs. Priestman & Lazenby and built by Quibell Ltd. From the washing of used bottles to the capping of filled ones the production process was completely automatic, giving a product untouched by hand. Clover had formerly operated from Nile Street.

FEBRUARY.

6th   Hull people were stunned by the news, announced from Sandringham, that the King had died peacefully in his sleep. Flags were flown at half mast on business premises, dances and concerts were speedily cancelled or postponed and the demand for black armbands caught outfitters by surprise. People were seen weeping openly in the streets as if overcome by a sense of personal loss. Two days later the accession of the new Queen Elizabeth was proclaimed from the Guildhall balcony at 3 p.m. by the Lord Mayor, Alderman R.E. Smith. A silent procession representing all aspects of Hull life then made its way to the City Hall where the message was repeated after a fanfare by Hull City Police Band. To coincide with the King's funeral on 15th, a Civic Service was held at Holy Trinity Church. Maroons were fired from Victoria Pier at 2 p.m. and works sirens sounded to mark the start of two minutes silence and a great hush descended over the city. Shops were closed, traffic came to a halt and schoolchildren, bus crews, factory workers, dockers and trawlermen all joined in the universal tribute.

12th   The Archbishop of Sweden consecrated the new **Swedish Church** at Drypool, a multi-purpose church/mission designed by Messrs. Horth & Andrew and built by F. Singleton & Sons Ltd. to serve the spiritual and recreational needs of residents and seamen alike. The building contained some beautiful woodwork, all the fittings and furnishings having come from Scandinavia.

19th Fire raged for nearly an hour on the top floor of the G.P.O. in Lowgate severing the city's trunk telephone links with the rest of Britain for the morning. Worst inconvenienced was the fish trade with merchants unable to find out what supplies their inland customers wanted. The demand for telegrams soared as a result.

The City Engineer's staff were busy on an unusual task, adapting a blitzed house in Coltman Street to make it even more 'war damaged' than before. It was to be Hull's Civil Defence training ground where volunteers would learn practical rescue techniques among broken walls, cracked floorboards, voids and debris.

MARCH.

9th The new **Finnish Church** was opened and dedicated by the Bishop of Mikkeli assisted by the Bishop of Hull. Like its Swedish counterpart next door it comprised a social centre on the ground floor and a 70 seat church above, replacing an earlier church completed in 1938 and destroyed by a bomb just four years later.

12th Hull's Stipendiary Magistrate, Mr. J.R. MacDonald, well-known to many as 'Mac', retired after 27 years distinguished service. The court was packed with civic leaders, police and court officials, and members of the public for his 'farewell' session.

13th Dr. Donald Soper, renowned for his controversial open air oratory, was the guest speaker at the 81st anniversary of Bourne Methodist Church, Anlaby Road. He had just completed 25 years preaching on London's Tower Hill.

There was a wave of protest from shopkeepers and others at a proposal to re-route inward buses from North Hull via Ferensway instead of Prospect Street and Jameson Street, which they claimed would affect trade and make staff late for work. Even more controversy was caused by a new Transport Committee ruling that inward buses must stop at the first stage until all fares had been collected, a move intended to tighten up on fare dodging. One councillor complained it had taken 20 minutes to ride from Stanhope Avenue to Durham Street. The unpopular rule was quickly rescinded.

The Welfare Services Committee voted to continue the weekly one-ounce tobacco allowance for the elderly men moving to Kingston Villas from the Beverley Road Hostel. Ald. J.D.L. Nicholson said,

"If they are used to smoking we should be the last people on earth to deprive them of that pleasure."

APRIL.

4th A new £10,000 **Dockers Medical Centre** on King George Dock was opened by Mr. Alfred Howell of the National Dock Labour Board. Board Chairman Lord Crook said the idea was inspired by Ernest Bevin, "an old friend whom they all knew and loved." One of 32 in Britain, it was not merely a first aid post but was specially designed with baths and a full range of therapeutic facilities.

26th The silver-haired soccer maestro, Raich Carter, played his last league match for Hull City at Doncaster. Hull needed one point to avoid relegation and the Tigers obliged by winning 1-0. On 28th Carter played in a home friendly drawn 2-2 against his first club Sunderland. After the game many of the 29,274 fans swarmed across the pitch and gathered in front of the directors' box chanting 'We want Raich' for 15 minutes.

28th Recruiting for the re-formed Home Guard began slowly at Park Street Barracks. Hull was to have two battalions with a combined strength of 1,800.

29th **Grange County Primary School**, the first of three new schools to serve the Bilton Grange estate, opened after the Easter holidays. As an experiment, to avoid using scarce traditional materials needed for housebuilding, it was constructed of prefabricated aluminium, producing a very light and airy building.

To improve the cleaning of double-decker buses at the Central Garage, Corporation Transport engineers had built their own bus washing machine, by studying an American leaflet, after the General Manager (Mr. G.H. Pulfrey) had seen one in operation in Chicago. It was the first of its type in Britain. Buses were driven at walking pace between two vertical revolving brushes heavily charged with water and then sprayed with more water to rinse them clean.

A chapter in local history closed on the fall of a gavel at an auction sale conducted by W.E. Lewendon & Sons. The property sold, No.2 Kingston Square, was where towards the end of last century Madame Emily Maria Clapham had employed 150 girls in her workrooms and put Hull on the fashion map by making gowns for society ladies and the monarchs of Europe. After her death in January at the age of 96, the coat of arms and sign in the hallway 'By

Hull's principal industries spent the early-1950s recovering productive capacity lost in the war. By mid-1952 J. Rank's new Clarence Flour Mills at Drypool towered high above the River Hull and were fully operational. Grain was taken from vessels moored alongside using the suction apparatus on the side of the silo. Photograph by courtesy of Innes Studios, Hessle.

Jordans, one of the best-known names locally for cycles and motorcycles, opened their modern showrooms in Story Street in 1952. At Christmas time children from far and wide would flock there to view the model railway and toy displays. Photograph by courtesy of Hull City Record Office.

appointment to H.M. Queen Maud of Norway' had been taken down and returned to Oslo. Madam Clapham's neice Mrs Emily Wall was continuing the business from the larger house next door and No.2 was sold to a timber firm for £3075.

MAY.

8th   Eleven years to the day since the cruel destruction of their original 'new' building, **Jordans of Hull's** rebuilt showrooms in Story Street were opened for business. Designed by Messrs. Roper Spencer & Hall on simple, modern lines and built by Stan Spruit in red rustic bricks relieved with artificial stone, the four-storey premises housed an impressive stock of motorcycles, mopeds, scooters and cycles as well as extensive departments for accessories and spare parts. The first floor Toy Department with its Triang, Hornby, Meccano and Trix products was to become a mecca for Hull schoolchildren especially at Christmas time. As if spurred on by friendly rivalry, several major building projects were suddenly nearing completion at about the same time. **Festival House** was ready to open and **Edwin Davis's** and **Hammonds** almost finished, while the Ravenseft building (now to be called **Queens House**) was giving new dignity to the spacious thoroughfares of Waterworks Street and King Edward Street.

8th   The City Council elections were the most crucial since the war with the possibility of the anti-Socialist Municipal Association Group (MAG) seizing control after nearly seven years of Labour rule. However there turned out to be little public interest and, contrary to expectations, Labour actually increased their strength.

16th   A large crowd of shoppers gathered in Paragon Square to hear American comedian and star of radio and stage, Dick Bentley, declare open the first phase of **Hammonds'** splendid new department store. Mr. James Powell (chairman) spoke of the 130 year history of the firm which had occupied the site since 1916. Bathed in brilliant sunshine for the event, the Portland stone and glass fronted structure was built mainly of reinforced concrete in order to economise on steel. The main contractors were Sir Robert McAlpine & Sons working to designs by London architects T.P. Bennett and Partners. Only the basement, ground and first floors at the Ferensway end were finished but demolition work was about to begin for stage two (the South Street end). Meanwhile temporary premises in West Street were retained for the hardware, gardening and footwear departments.

16th   Hepworths tailoring shop became one of the first businesses to open at **Queens House** quickly followed by gent's outfitters S.M. Bass.

21st   The Rt. Rev. Bishop G. Brunner, Bishop of Elide, opened the new **Catholic Church of St. Joseph**, Boothferry Road, after its conversion from some old farm buildings by volunteers from the parish.

Gifts of birds from local breeders allowed the aviaries at East and Pickering Parks to be stocked up again for the first time since the war, much to the delight of Hull children.

JUNE.

1st   **The Marine Café** at Victoria Pier, designed by the City Architect with an unusual 'piano-curve' frontage, was opened by the Civic Catering Committee in time for the Whit Sunday trade.

4th   **Edwin Davis & Co. Ltd.** commenced trading in their newly built Bond Street department store. The firm, a household name locally, was founded in 1790 on the Labour Exchange site in Market Place and bombed in a Zeppelin raid in 1915. After creating one of Hull's finest stores in Bond Street they were unlucky enough to be blitzed again in the raids of May 1941. The new store was designed by F.J. Horth & H. Andrew and built by Spooners (Hull) Ltd. in Ibstock brick with cast stone window surrounds and steel sashes typical of the period.

8th   Bilton Grange residents welcomed their first bus service. For the first four years the no. 58 operated along Barham Road to the end of Nestor Grove as a branch of route 48, until the strengthening of Marfleet Lane bridge permitted a more direct service.

21st   Admiral Sir Robert Burnett (chairman of the White Fish Authority) officially opened the Royal National Mission to Deep Sea Fishermen's **Queen Mary Hostel** in Goulton Street. The £30,000 hostel had 15 'cabins' available for use by fishermen during the turnround of Hull trawlers together with a room for social and religious gatherings, a sick bay and a place for drying fishing gear. A 70 ft. long mural painted by Miss Field of Hessle depicted the evolution of fishing vessels through the centuries. Hull was the first port to have new local headquarters, which superseded a makeshift building in the Boulevard. The architects were Elsworth, Sykes & Partners and building contractors J. Mather & Son.

The spring of 1952 saw a spate of 'openings' as the first batch of reconstruction projects reached fruition. The new Edwin Davis store marked the beginning of the redevelopment of Bond Street, one of Hull's oldest shopping streets. Photograph by courtesy of Innes Studios, Hessle.

Shoppers in Paragon Square sharing a joke with American comedian Dick Bentley as he prepares to cut the tape to open the first stage of Hammonds new department store on 16th May, 1952. Photograph by courtesy of Innes Studios, Hessle.

Admiral Sir Robert Burnett opening the Queen Mary Hostel in Goulton Street on 21st June, 1952. The hostel's purpose was to offer a bed and hospitality to men from out of town who were working on Hull trawlers and unable to get home in the 72 hour or five tides interval between docking and sailing. Photograph by courtesy of the Royal National Mission to Deep Sea Fishermen.

Probation officer David Banks had the idea of forming a Hull Boys Barge Club in an attempt to reduce the amount of damage being caused to port property by youths who couldn't resist the lure of dockland. The Docks Board gave local youngsters their own adventure craft, which was named the 'Marjorie Bailey' by the Lord Mayor. After renovation the barge was moored in the Humber Dock basin and used by club members to sample all kinds of activities connected with sailing and the sea.

The Corporation found the first tenants for their showpiece project, **Festival House** in Jameson Street. J.H. Robinson (Hull) Ltd. of Anlaby Road opened a tools and hardware shop and the Co-operative Insurance Society moved into the offices above.

Mr. Bob Jackson, manager of First Division team Portsmouth since 1947, became Hull City's new manager. The former inside-forward's fashion for wearing a bow tie was soon copied by many Boothferry Park regulars. In contrast to the Carter era his time at Hull was a gloomy one, the team achieving little on the field of play.

JULY.

1st   Twenty-one engineers were engaged on a big operation to convert the city's 343 public telephone boxes to take twopenny calls. Following a Telephones Committee resolution Hull ceased to be the only place in the country with penny-a-call phone boxes in a move calculated to bring in an extra £12-13,000 a year.

16th   The Parks & Burials Committee decided to allow Sunday football on Corporation pitches after turning a blind eye for years. Corner flags and whistles would not be permitted however. Councillor A. Parker said "We must not be narrow minded about these things, we must be progressive."

18th   Northern Clothing Co. (Hull) Ltd. opened a new walk-through store at 44-6 Ferensway and 40-2 Brook Street. The building, known as 'Block 41A' or **Brook Chambers**, had just been completed, filling a gap in Ferensway's impressive neo-Georgian eastern facade. Northern had been bombed out of 67 King Edward Street, their home since 1923.

21st   Norman Collier of Lockwood Street, a young comedian in Hull's BBC Top Town broadcast team, began his professional career at the Tivoli Theatre where Jimmy Young was top of the bill. The former building trade worker was also booked to appear at the City Varieties, Leeds.

21st   Barclays Bank opened a branch in Paragon Square following the partial-restoration of **Seatons Buildings** behind the war memorial. Although Ancaster stone was specified for the ground floor, spending restrictions dictated the use of plain brick for the upper storeys, a style that outraged the critics of modern architecture for such a prestige site.

Work was progressing well on rebuilding the **Central Bus Garage**. Workmen were busy assembling the first of four 150 ft. long lattice girders to support the roof which was then raised into place using hand winches. The garage had been wrecked by a landmine and 43 motorbuses destroyed.

AUGUST.

1st   Waterworks Street, the short thoroughfare at the side of the City Hall and boarding point for the Anlaby Road and Hessle Road trolleybuses, was officially renamed Paragon Street.

30th   A service that had operated as a public amenity since 1939 was closed down because of waning support. In their heyday the motor ambulances run by the St. John Ambulance Brigade had done 3,000 hours of duty a year staffed mainly by volunteers and charging only a nominal fee. Wartime work had included removing bed-ridden people from bomb-damaged homes and distributing clothing and comforts to rest centres. Until 1948 St. John's had been the only 24 hour service in the city apart from the police ambulances used for street accidents and sudden illnesses. The decline set in when the new National Health Service introduced a modern fleet of ambulances with a large paid staff of drivers and attendants. The Brigade proposed to retain two ambulances as mobile first aid posts for sports events.

All over Hull air raid sirens were being re-erected by the British Electricity Authority as part of the nation's precautions against hostilities. Some were on factory premises such as Reckitt's and the National Radiator works; others were located at the Guildhall, Sculcoates Power Station, Priory Cinema, East Hull Fire Station and other landmarks. From time to time they were tested for audibility after suitable public warning had been given in the newspapers.

SEPTEMBER.

7th   Tens of thousands of onlookers lined the route between Ferensway and Scarborough's Marine Drive as 94 veteran cars took part in the biggest rally to date organised by the North-Eastern section of the Veteran Car Club, an annual event fast rivalling the famous London to Brighton 'old crocks' race.

12th   At a crowded ceremony the Archbishop of York consecrated **St. Philip's Church** on Barham Road, the first replacement for one of the blitzed city centre churches to be built on an entirely new site. A plain looking dual-purpose church cum social hall, its role was to serve the Bilton Grange district of the parish of Marfleet.   The furnishings came from the old St. Philip's Church in George Street. The widow of Canon Sedgwick, who had been killed by falling masonry while firewatching there, was present for the ceremony. Teams of lay people from many of Hull's churches had visited the young estate's 1,500 homes to tell residents of the facilities.

What was claimed to be the largest crane of its kind in the country was working in the city centre.   The 80 ft. high jib was helping to erect the steel framework for phase two of the **Queens House** development, lifting loads of up to five tons at a time.

Hull trawler owners decided to withdraw landing facilities from Icelandic trawlers after Iceland unilaterally extended her territorial limits to four miles, thereby excluding British vessels from 5,000 square miles of first-class fishing grounds which she claimed were being over-fished. Britain did not accept the extension until 1956.

There was news of a £950,000 plan by the British Transport Commission to replace 45 of the original cranes on King George Dock with modern six ton versions with double the lifting speed, over a 3-4 year period. The idea was to speed up the turnround of ships, especially the big Australian and American vessels now using the port. The dock's mains electricity supply was also to be modernised and converted from DC to AC and work had already begun on a 21-month contract to rebuild No. 12 Quay.

OCTOBER.

4th   At 11.20 a.m. Portishead radio picked up an S.O.S. message indicating that the Hull trawler *Norman* (H289) was in trouble. The 629 ton Northern Fishing Company vessel was wrecked in thick fog on a desolate rocky island near Cape Farewell off the southern tip of Greenland. The 20-strong crew leapt overboard but only one succeeded in reaching the shore safely. Norman Spencer, 19 year old deckie learner, was picked up next morning by a Norwegian salvage ship. The entire Hessle Road community was plunged into mourning and flags were flown at half-mast from boats and the Fish

Dock offices. The heartbreaking task of delivering the bleak news to the families fell to Pastor Tom Chappell and his wife Elsie who had been preparing for harvest festival at the Fishermen's Bethel. For five hours they went from home to home comforting the bereaved. The Lord Mayor opened a fund for the dependants and it was decided to hold a special midnight matinee at the Tivoli, the fishermen's favourite theatre. The artists appearing there - Nat Mills & Bobbie, the Kordites, Billy Thorburn and Terry Scott - gave their services free and raised £360 by staging a mini-auction.

10th   Two distinguished visitors came to Hull: H.R.H. The Princess Royal called at the British Legion headquarters in Beverley Road (which as Princess Mary she had opened in 1926) and then proceeded to Hotham Road South for the opening of **Arthur Shepherd Court** (the Earl Haig Homes), so named in tribute to the magnificent work of Mr. Shepherd, a founder patron of the Legion in Hull and ex-Lord Mayor. The Princess took tea at Trinity House and spent some time at the Newland Sailors Children's Homes before leaving the city. As the Princess departed, the Deputy Prime Minister Mr. Anthony Eden was arriving for an evening engagement at the City Hall, pausing at North Hull Conservative Federation's Princes Avenue headquarters en route. The building was named Eden House in his honour.

17th   Second floor rooms were gutted and much valuable equipment destroyed in an early morning fire at the Municipal Technical College in Park Street.

27th   Workmen began filling in a giant hole in the ground in front of Hammonds new store. The eyesore had remained after the store was built while the Corporation and the firm negotiated over who was responsible for the plot of ground.

28th   Hull's old-established Literary & Philosophical Society (known colloquially as the Lit. & Phil.) began meeting in the new 750 seater hall above Hammonds. Some of the lecture topics lined up give an interesting insight into the burning issues of the day: "British Commonwealth - Is it withering away?"; "Obstacles to a united Germany"; "Problems of Booms and Slumps"; "Development and use of Atomic Energy", and "The Soviet Union."

Unsightly street scenes with lines of overhead telephone wires running from pole to pole were destined to disappear as the Telephones Department embarked on major extensions to their underground cable network. Many of the existing cables had reached the limit of their capacity and so there was little option but

Father Christmas helped to bring national recognition to Hull in 1952 when he 'took up residence' at the Mytongate Telephone Exchange. For three nights callers from all over Britain crowded the switchboard to hear his festive story. Photograph by courtesy of Innes Studios, Hessle.

The formation of a Hull Boys Barge Club gave 1950s teenagers the chance to learn sailing techniques and dream of a life on the ocean wave. An old iron hulk, restored to former glory, was moored near the Pier. Photograph by courtesy of Innes Studios, Hessle.

to go underground. In future there would simply be a series of poles with lines running to the houses like a spider's web.

NOVEMBER.

11th Dr. Hugh Webster, Hull's first Labour Alderman and the oldest practising doctor in the city, died at his Anlaby Road home aged 85.

The Corporation took over a large block of property in Witham in the process of being converted from the derelict furniture and carpet store of E. Shaw & Son. The Central Purchasing Department was transferred there from Hessle Road while next door the Maternal & Child Health Services were relocating from Hanover Square to make way for a new Guildhall boiler house.

Nearly 200 Hull structures of special architectural or historic interest were 'listed' by the Minister of Housing & Local Government to protect them from being demolished or altered without consent. The list included the Church Institute, Haworth Hall, the Charterhouse, Wilberforce House, the old Grammar School, Ye Olde White Harte public house and the King William III statue. Although conservation was perhaps not such a talking point as it is today, there was great concern when it looked as though the war-damaged Master's House at Hull Charterhouse would have to be pulled down. The Lord Mayor called a conference of interested parties and there were demands for special measures to prevent buildings such as this from falling down through neglect.

Traders and planners were bitterly disappointed at Hull's £400,000 capital allocation for reconstruction work in 1953. They had hoped for a much bigger share of the £4.5m. available for the 18 blitzed cities. Thornton Varleys and Bladons in particular were angry that their store rebuilding plans were pushed back yet again.

DECEMBER.

5th The **Humber Laboratory**, a new Fisheries Research Station in Wassand Street, was officially opened by Sir Ben Lockspeiser, secretary to the Department of Scientific & Industrial Research. Its role was to carry out studies into the preservation of fish for the food industry.

22nd A new service that was to put Hull firmly on the map for years to come was inaugurated by the Telephones Department after an idea suggested by Councillor J.M. Stamper was successfully tested.

It allowed children from far and wide to dial a Hull number and listen to a message from Father Christmas. News of the innovation rapidly spread and soon calls were coming in from all over Britain to the only city boasting a 'telephone link' to Santa Claus. The three minute recording included carols recorded in Holy Trinity Church and a Christmas story from Santa's reindeer. Initially 20 lines were made available on Hull Central 32800 between 5 and 8 p.m. but the demand was such that extra lines and more staff had to be hastily arranged. Over the three nights more than 18,000 calls came in from as far away as Guernsey, Glasgow and Portsmouth, exceeding all expectations and providing ample justification for making the service an annual feature. The following year the number of calls doubled.

29th Gracie Fields, the 'Lancashire Lass' who had become one of the world's best-loved entertainers, delighted a capacity audience at a charity concert at the City Hall. Gracie had a special affection for Hull which had been one of her early stepping stones to fame.

NEW HOUSES COMPLETED.			
	Corporation	Private	Total
1950	535	108	643
1951	1076	64	1140
1952	1167	73	1240
1953	909	71	980
1954	917	78	995
1955	730	120	850
1956	850	94	944
1957	863	80	943
1958	1108	112	1220
1959	810	140	950

Information by courtesy of Hull City Council.

BUILDING NEW COMMUNITIES.

In the 1950s Hull faced housing needs of enormous proportions, the post-war marriage boom and a general property shortage having pushed the Corporation-house waiting list past the 16,000 mark. To tackle these problems sufficient land was reserved in the City Development Plan to build homes for 56,000 people - 37,000 on 'green field' sites and 19,000 on land currently occupied by unfit property.

Initially the main thrust of the Corporation's building programme was on the eastern fringes of the city where the first major deep drainage scheme was nearing completion. Three large estates were planned: Bilton Grange, Longhill and Greatfield. But instead of repeating the sprawling, straggling layouts of pre-war days with little variety of house types and few amenities, it was decided to follow the ideas in Abercrombie's futuristic 'Plan for Hull' and build in 'neighbourhood units' - each a self-contained community with its own schools, shops, churches, health centres and other services within easy reach of all the residents and free from disturbance by heavy traffic and industry.

By 1952 work was well under way on the first of the three, Bilton Grange. Extending over 340 acres between Holderness High Road and Hopewell Road, it had a very spacious feel to it with unfenced front gardens, lots of large grassed areas, wide roads lined with verges and massive roundabouts. Moreover, the City Architect (Mr. Andrew Rankine) produced an imaginative range of 2, 3 and 4-bedroom houses, flats, maisonettes and old people's bungalows in various styles - some in rows, some L-shaped, others grouped around paved court yards and so on - to create a varied, interesting streetscape. Altogether around 2,500 dwellings were planned to house nearly 9,000 people. Many of the early tenants were young families who had been living with relatives for some time, thrilled at the prospect of their first home. For the elderly too there was a chance to move to somewhere more compact thereby releasing a house elsewhere for another family.

Knitting together a new community the size of a small town proved to be no easy task, especially as the promised social facilities failed at first to keep pace with the houses. Early tenants had to be content with mobile shops for their daily needs and faced a 20-minute walk to Holderness Road to collect their pensions. The Tenants and Families Association (which organised meetings, socials, dances, P.T. and needlework classes at Hopewell Road School as well as football for the youngsters and an advice bureau) did help people get to know one another and share their problems. Some of their concerns were well-aired when the T.F.A. arranged an 'Any Questions?' night in October, 1952. Residents bombarded their councillors with complaints about the lack of shops, phone boxes, surgeries, lock up garages etc. and the poor bus service. They were equally fed up with chasing children and dogs from their front gardens as a result of the Corporation's 'no fences' policy, which was said to be partly for aesthetic reasons and partly to do with the cost of timber. Gradually though these teething troubles were sorted out and Bilton Grange did become a popular place to live.

In the summer of 1952 work began on the roads and sewers for the Longhill estate, enabling the first houses to be erected in August 1953. This community was to the north of Holderness High Road and Saltshouse Road. Unlike Bilton Grange which had been a featureless plain, the area had many fine trees and hedges which could be retained and built around to give the estate a pleasant rural character. About 2,200 homes were planned in similar styles to those on Bilton Grange.

The first thousand houses of the third estate, Greatfield, were started by the end of 1954. Situated at the far eastern end of Preston Road (and thereby preventing it from ever reaching the destination implied by its name) it was built on agricultural land with a variety of former owners including Trinity House and St. John's College, Cambridge. A total of 2,410 houses were to be built by 1961, many of the tenants coming from the streets of Holderness Road and Hessle Road affected by the Council's Clearance Programme which was just getting into its stride. They too faced problems adjusting to a new life 'in the east', especially the Hessle Road fishing folk uprooted from their beloved community, but apparently the estate soon developed a great sense of neighbourliness.

After about 1957 the focus of building switched to Central and West Hull. In the area between Hessle Road, Anlaby Road and Bean Street redevelopment of a different kind was in progress. A new neighbourhood was being created by making a clean sweep of the old streets and removing the chaotic mixture of damp, decaying houses, factories, back-street workshops and bomb sites. There were plans to move 91 firms out of the area (many to be relocated in the Waverley Street/Lister Street area south of Hessle Road) and to reduce the number of shops and licensed premises in line with modern needs. Eventually around 8,000 people would find themselves living in a pleasant environment.

Newly-occupied houses on the Bricknell Avenue Corporation housing estate. The mobile grocer was a welcome visitor before permanent shops were provided. Photograph by courtesy of Hull City Record Office.

Housing in Hull

The complex road layout on the new East Hull estates necessitated the provision of a street map at the entrance to guide visitors and delivery people. Photograph by Harry Cartlidge.

Wakefield Street, showing the railway stables on the right. Inner city residents often lived side by side with factories, workshops or depots with their attendant traffic dangers, noise, smells and grime. Children played in the street because there was nowhere else to go. The 1951 Development Plan and slum clearance programme aimed to eradicate these problems. Photograph by courtesy of Hull City Council Department of Planning and Design.

These six-storey blocks in Porter Street, completed by late-1956, were Hull's first tall flats. Later they were dwarfed by 12-storey blocks nearby and some even higher along Anlaby Road as a severe land shortage forced the Corporation to build skywards. Photograph by courtesy of Hull City Council Department of Planning and Design.

NRH 101, the prototype 'Coronation' trolleybus undergoing trials in Cottingham Road. Designed for one man operation (but never so used), the Coronations were perhaps the most unusual buses ever to grace the streets of Hull. They were not universally popular: Passengers tended to get trapped in the doors and swept off their feet by the powerful acceleration! Photograph by courtesy of Kingston upon Hull City Transport Ltd.

1953

The year that:-

Marshal Joseph Stalin the Soviet Leader died aged 74.

Edmund Hillary and Sherpa Tenzing were the first to conquer the summit of Mount Everest (29,002 ft.).

H.M. Queen Elizabeth II was crowned in Westminster Abbey.

The Korean Armistice was signed at Panmunjom.

A link between smoking and lung cancer was first established.

Ian Fleming introduced James Bond in the book 'Casino Royale'.

Three hundred died and thousands were made homeless when freak floods swamped Canvey Island.

JANUARY.

10th Relatives and friends of the 470 office staff of **Reckitt & Colman Ltd.** were invited to view the firm's new offices and directors' suite, completed after two years work on the Dansom Lane site. The four-storey post-war style building brought all the staff together in warm, spacious, well-lit accommodation after years of coping in temporary huts and old chapels nearby. In the forecourt was an ornamental garden with a memorial to Hull's pioneer industrialist and benefactor Sir James Reckitt.

19th The newly-installed Boothferry Park floodlights were used for the first time in public. Hull City played in fog before a 31,700 crowd, losing 1-4 to Dundee. Artificial lighting was not approved for league matches until 1956 but City lined up a series of evening friendlies against leading British and Continental sides in a bid to attract those, such as shop workers, unable to support Saturday games. The lights, supported on two gantries above the covered stands, were considered to be among the best in the country.

23rd The safest and most modern trolleybus invented, Sunbeam 'Coronation' class vehicle 101 (NRH 101), entered service with Hull Corporation on the no. 61 Chanterlands Avenue route after being the centre of attention at London's 1952 Commercial Motor Show. The 54-seat double-decker, built by Charles Roe Ltd. of Leeds, had many features setting it apart from Hull's existing trolleybuses:
- twin doors (controlled by the driver and power interlocked to prevent the bus moving while they were open),
- a double staircase to reduce delays at stops,
- American-style trolley retrievers to arrest dewired trolleys, and
- smoother, automatic acceleration.

The Transport Committee later resolved to purchase 15 similar vehicles which came into service by 1955.

26th The Lord Mayor saw first-hand evidence of the recent rapid development of one of Hull's leading firms, **Smith & Nephew Ltd.** (surgical dressing manufacturers) when he paid a visit to open a new railway siding leading into their covered loading bay. Rebuilding of the Tadman Street side of the factory had been completed last August and work was now under way on the Jackson Street frontage.

30th It was announced that the Debenhams organisation, owners of 110 mainly high-class drapery shops, had acquired a controlling interest in Thornton Varley Ltd. of Prospect Street. Mr. Arthur Thornton Varley, whose father founded the well-known Hull store in 1870, continued to serve as company chairman until his death in March.

After studying the City Engineer's costings the Baths Committee recommended deferring indefinitely the provision of an ice skating rink for Hull. A rink had been proposed for Albert Avenue but it was thought the Ministry would be unlikely to approve such a costly scheme with the economy in its present state.

Another large-scale block development contributing to the revival of Hull's central shopping area was about to take shape. Hoardings were being erected around the vacant land bounded by King Edward Street, Savile Street and Jameson Street to allow foundation work to begin on a £250,000 four-storey shops and offices project for the **Triangle Development Trust**. The scheme was believed to be unique in that it represented a co-operative effort, by the traders who had previously occupied the site and the Corporation, to re-develop an area themselves on a mixed freehold and leasehold basis. Only a small portion of the original Jameson Street buildings would be retained; others including Dolcis corner and the old Sloanes Billiard Hall would be rebuilt in a uniform style designed by the architects, Messrs. Gelder & Kitchen, to harmonise with Queens House opposite.

It was a boom period for the advertising poster industry. Every vacant space seemed to be covered with hoardings proclaiming the latest products or cinema shows. They either brightened up the drab streets in an age of austerity or created an eyesore, depending on your point of view. Schemes to remove them from the main roads began in 1954. Photograph by courtesy of Hull City Council Department of Planning and Design.

The former Beverley Road Wesleyan Chapel, opposite Brunswick Avenue, lay in ruins after a fierce blaze in 1953. Flames shot 120 feet into the air and 35 men with 15 jets, including one on a 100ft. turntable ladder, were required to bring the incident under control. Photograph by courtesy of Sam Allon Collection.

The Public Libraries Committee planned to introduce a Technical Inter-loan Service so that firms and researchers could pool the resources of their various libraries. Mutual access would be available to thousands of specialist publications that were too costly for the Reference Library to buy.

FEBRUARY.

1st   A weekend of severe gales along the east coast brought havoc to Hull. Walls, TV aerials, chimneys and hoardings were torn down and there were floods in the Old Town with water reaching a depth of 5-6 ft. in cellars in Lowgate. The Lord Mayor opened a fund for the Canvey Island flood disaster and several churches made house-to-house collections to provide comforts for the victims.

5th   Mr. H.F. Alston was appointed Town Planning Officer in succession to Mr. Aylmer Coates who had moved to Lancashire. Over the next 20 years Mr. Alston was to play a key role in helping to shape Hull's redevelopment.

Talk of the rates increasing by 2/- in the pound to 27/- prompted a revival of the Hull Ratepayers League. A protest meeting held at the Y.P.I. called on the City Council to revise its estimates and take steps to progressively reduce the rates burden over the next three years. The League had been a lively force before the war and once succeeded in turning a 1/6 increase into a reduction of 2d. in the pound. Mr. Harry Birtles of Alexandra Road was its general secretary. With public interest thus stirred, at the Council meeting on 5th March the galleries were filled to capacity with citizens keen to hear the debate. Councillor Leo Schultz (Leader of the Council and Finance Committee Chairman) explained that the spending plans of four committees - Education, Housing, Town Planning and Works - were largely responsible for the increased costs and, given the scale of redevelopment Hull faced, higher rates were unavoidable. There were still more than 15,000 people waiting for houses and a desperate need for new schools (pupil intake having risen by 5,000 in two years) as well as a long-term commitment to a £7 million main drainage scheme. The Council approved the 27/- rate.

One of Hull's oldest streets was about to disappear as building work progressed. Barriers were placed across the northern part of Chariot Street to allow the next 'leg' of **Queens House** to be started and a car park laid out in the centre. The street was believed to date back to the 16th century and be so named because it was a chariot route to the old walled town of Hull. It had been a popular shopping street until left in ruins by the blitz.

The Health Committee decided to dispose of the **Evan Fraser Hospital** at Sutton. Opened in 1899 as a smallpox isolation centre it last saw service as a wartime outpost for the inmates of the Anlaby Road and Beverley Road Institutions. Later it was kept in reserve in case of an epidemic. The buildings were demolished in 1958.

MARCH.

9th   A disastrous early morning fire occurred at White & Farrell Ltd.'s print works on Beverley Road putting 50 employees out of a job. Only the shell and spires remained of the building which had opened in 1862 as Beverley Road Wesleyan Church and played a prominent role in Hull's church life until its closure in 1941. The congregation had once included some well-known local business leaders including the grocer, Wm. Jackson.

24th   Dancers at the City Hall were among the first to hear the news of the death of Queen Mary. The Lord Mayor left the stage to take a telephone call and a short period of silence was observed. Next day special prayers were said at Newland High School which the late Queen had opened during a visit to Hull in 1914.

28th   A dedication ceremony was held at the new **East Hull Congregational Church** at the corner of James Reckitt Avenue and Clifford Avenue. The Rev. Trevor Roberts (Hull & East Riding District Secretary) knocked on the door which was ceremonially opened by Mrs E. Sproxton. Building of the church, designed by Mr. A.P. Taylor, had been severely delayed by a steel shortage caused by the re-armament programme.

Two dozen blue and white police boxes, a familiar sight at many Hull street corners, were being phased out following the introduction of improved methods of police communication, using '99' calls and wireless patrol cars. Larger 'section boxes' were being erected at strategic points such as Calvert Lane, Staveley Road and Holderness Road and extra telephone cabinets (permanently connected to a divisional police station) fixed to lamp standards so that people could easily call the police in an emergency.

APRIL.

1st   The Deputy Lord Mayor, Alderman Ralph Smith, died suddenly aged 57. An ardent worker for hospital and health services, he had chaired the Health Committee for many years. Only the day before, his final duty had been to open **Hugh Webster House** in St. Luke's Street, Hull Corporation's first purpose-built home for the elderly. Built by E. Barker Ltd., it would become home to 30 people.

12th Chipperfields Circus parade, passing through the streets from English Street Goods Station to Walton Street, where the Big Top was about to open for two weeks, provided a treat for Hull's youngsters. Headed by the 2nd Battalion Army Cadet Corps from Cottingham it included 16 elephants, dozens of horses, ponies, camels, llamas, cowboys, clowns and a Roman chariot, with scores of children tacked on behind. Crowds ten deep in places thronged the route and the queues waiting at bus stops to go into town put such a strain on the public transport system that buses had to be hurriedly switched from the quieter routes.

16th Two loud explosions heralded a spectacular fire that caused £20,000 worth of damage to Beecroft & Wightman Ltd.'s wood flour factory in Burleigh Street. The incident scared the occupants of adjoining houses, one of whom was blown out of bed by the blast.

19th Over a thousand relatives watched the Lord Mayor unveil a memorial to Hull's civilian casualties of the war. Designed by the City Architect, the simple yet dignified structure was set in a semi-circular court of raised flower beds. Local representatives of every walk of civilian and military life wearing robes, uniforms and medals joined the pilgrimage to the Northern Cemetery for a wreath laying service led by the Bishop of Hull. Afterwards a long line of citizens filed past the memorial and laid their own floral tributes.

24th A group of bible students known as Christadelphians who had met in Hull since 1901 but never had their own rooms, held their first lecture in a hall they had built for themselves in St. Ninian's Walk.

27th A new venue where railwaymen and their families could meet socially, the **Paragon Institute** in Anlaby Road, was opened by Mr. H.A. Short, Chief Regional Officer (North Eastern Region) supported by the Institute President Mr. S.A. Finnis. A concert by Hull Railwaymen's Silver Band quartet followed. The clubrooms were converted from an old reception centre for foreign immigrants and replaced temporary premises at Dairycoates.

28th The Astronomer Royal, Sir Harold Spencer Jones, opened an observatory at Kingston High School. An initiative of headmaster Dr. Cameron Walker who was keenly interested in astronomy, it led to the formation of a Hull & East Riding Astronomical Association.

MAY.

3rd Former Prime Minister Mr. Clement Attlee was given a rapturous welcome on entering the City Hall to speak to 1,600 Labour Movement supporters at their May Day celebrations. It was the climax of one of the finest May Day demonstrations for years. Earlier, big crowds had gathered at Corporation Fields to hear speeches on Labour's aims and aspirations by local politicians and trade unionists Cmdr. Harry Pursey, Jack Foord, Alderman Bridges and Bert Hazell.

17th About 3,000 Scouts, Guides and members of other uniformed youth organisations marched through the city centre to the accompaniment of several bands after Youth Sunday services at local churches. The parade, bathed in brilliant sunshine, was one of the largest for many years and took 25 minutes to pass the Lord Mayor's saluting base in front of Ferens Art Gallery.

The first of many blue and white commemorative plaques, pointing out locations of historical interest to visitors, were placed on the site of the Beverley Gate, the former Queens Dock and the G.P.O. (the site of Henry VIII's Suffolk Palace).

JUNE.

2nd Hull celebrated the Coronation of Her Majesty Queen Elizabeth II (*see page 58*).

8th After a year's planning a scheme got under way to provide school crossing wardens at 48 points in the city to escort children across busy road junctions. An appeal for volunteers among people of pensionable age had resulted in a flood of applications. After receiving road safety training the chosen 40 men and eight women took up their duties four times a day for a fee of 1/6 a time. The wardens wore peaked caps and carried warning signs on poles, the shape of which soon gave rise to the nickname 'lollipop wardens'.

15th Councillors described the decision of Montague Burton Ltd. not to go ahead with a clothing factory on Hessle High Road as a tragedy for the city. The firm had planned to employ 2,000 mainly women workers and had pressed the Ministry for a building licence for nearly four years without success.

29th Dr. T.E.M. Tillyard, Master of Jesus College, Cambridge, officially opened the new premises of **Hull Grammar School** off Bricknell Avenue. It was the seventh site for the school which had

A touch of colour and fun was brought to the city centre when some raised flower beds were placed in front of Queens House sporting unusual displays of cacti and summer bedding plants. It was intended to be a temporary measure as plans had been drawn up to convert Paragon Street into a dual-carriageway. Photograph by courtesy of Harry Cartlidge.

a long and distinguished history dating back to the 14th century. The Leicester Street building from which it now moved had been inadequate for years. The new 700 pupil school, built by F. Hall & Sons Ltd., cost £235,000 and boasted the most modern facilities including science laboratories, art and music rooms, metal and woodwork shops and a well equipped gymnasium. One of the first events in the new hall was a drama production, 'The Happiest Days of Your Life'.

It was decided to extend the child immunisation programme by making vaccine available to all Hull children against whooping cough, probably one of the most infectious childhood diseases. The scheme had already succeeded in combating diptheria. For the first time since records began no cases had been reported for two years.

JULY.

1st   For the first time in the history of the service the 80 Humber pilots were on strike and ships were having to proceed into port without assistance. The men were in dispute with the Humber Conservancy Board.

3rd   A three-car diesel train with the appearance of a 'bus on rails' was undergoing trials on local passenger services to South Howden, Brough and Beverley.

8th   Hull Corporation were the main objectors at a public inquiry held at Hessle Town Hall into Haltemprice Urban District Council's petition for borough status. Created in 1935, Haltemprice adjoined Hull's western border and included the settlements of Cottingham, Willerby, Anlaby and Hessle. The city claimed it was too small to be a borough and depended on its larger neighbour for jobs, water supply, bus services and entertainments. Hull was looking to Haltemprice to re-house an overspill population of 15,000 over the next two decades and considered there was a strong case for incorporating it in the city.

14th   The Lord Mayor opened a temporary branch library for the tenants of Bilton Grange at Grange School, Barham Road. It opened three evenings a week and all day Saturday staffed by volunteer helpers from the Tenants and Families Association. After use the book stands could be rolled away to bring the school hall back into operation.

15th   A mobile column of 50 vehicles manned by 190 soldiers and RAF men swung into action in the biggest Civil Defence exercise

for eight years. 'Exercise Tiger' was set up to respond to an emergency created by the 'bombing' of central Hull with high explosives and incendiaries. Incidents were set up in derelict buildings and AFS personnel practised fire-fighting while the St. John Ambulance Brigade attended to the wounded. Next evening a big parade mustered in Queens Gardens to demonstrate Hull's Civil Defence strength to the public.

16th   Roman Catholics on Bilton Grange acquired a church of their own when the Bishop of Elide, Rt. Rev. G. Brunner, preached at the opening service of **St. Bede's** in Hopewell Road. Many of the furnishings were given by Sacred Heart parish where members had previously worshipped.

24th   After a 66 year life, the Beverley Road Secondary School for Boys closed down before merging with Wawne Street and Thomas Stratten Schools to form a new school known as **Wilberforce High** based at the old Grammar School buildings in Leicester Street.

24th   Work on 12 ships in King George Dock stopped during the afternoon when 2,000 dockers staged a mass walk off in support of a gang working on a maize ship, the *Argodon*. The dispute flared up when the men were forced to endure 115 degrees of heat while discharging maize into bags by the ancient hand-scuttle method, a job for which modern suction equipment was normally available. It was the first serious disruption at the port since 1945 and eventually 4,000 men were out and 51 ships lay idle. Three days later the men agreed to go back while negotiations progressed.

Phase two of **Queens House** was ready for occupation. Tenants taking shop units included Cavendish (furnishings), the Direct Raincoat Co., J. Hawkins & Sons Ltd. and Stylo (clothing), George Schonhut (pork butcher) and Balloon Stores. The last sold hardware, china and glass but were especially noted for their first-floor cake decoration department.

With the Grammar School established on a different site to that originally planned, Housing Committee members decided to find out whether residents of Grammar School Road would agree to a change of name. Meanwhile Bishop Alcock Road was the name chosen for the road leading to the new school, in tribute to its founder.

Dancing was still one of the most popular indoor pastimes. The City Hall was splendidly decorated for a Coronation Ball featuring the Norman Ashton Band. Photograph by courtesy of Innes Studios, Hessle.

The Leeds Arms in Porter Street was one of several public houses to pull their last pints in the 'fifties. As redevelopment of the area between Hessle Road and Anlaby Road progressed, its 31 licensed premises would eventually reduce to just four. Photograph by courtesy of Hull City Record Office.

HULL AT WORK : The growth of the paint trade in the city led to the establishment of metal can manufacture. Here women are fitting rims to paint tins for Sissons Paints with the aid of a machine.

A 1950s view across the packing room at the Gipsyville factory of the Metal Box Company Ltd., one of two in Hull turning out a variety of containers for paints, varnishes, oils, polishes and various food products.

Photographs by courtesy of Innes Studios, Hessle.

AUGUST.

1st   The Mother Humber Home for elderly women in Beverley Road was taken over by Hull Corporation and renamed **Rose Villa** after becoming too great a financial burden for the Mother Humber Fund that had opened it in 1947. The Fund now concentrated instead on providing clothing and grocery vouchers and Christmas gifts of coal for needy pensioners.

3rd   Unbroken sunshine and soaring temperatures encouraged record Bank Holiday crowds to desert Hull for the coast. There were long queues for buses and trains as an estimated 15,000 trippers headed for Bridlington and 5,000 each for Hornsea and Withernsea. Queens Gardens were packed with families playing on the lawns or watching the fountain while Corporation Pier, with the mobile theatre performing nearby, was a good place to cool down. Paull, Brough and Ferriby foreshores were popular places for those with cars.

31st   The new Anlaby Road premises of **Cornelius Parish Ltd.** were opened by Mr. C.S. Buckley, general sales manager of the Austin Motor Co. Ltd. Designed by Mr. R.G. Clark and built by Fenner Panton & Co. Ltd., they accommodated showrooms, offices, workshops, a parts department and a Regent petrol forecourt offering 24 hour/seven day service. The firm's garage had been destroyed in 1941 enforcing an 11 year absence from the city centre.

An 'attractive gift' was presented to the 100,000th patron to visit the New Theatre since its 1939 opening.

Reconstruction of **Thornton Varley's** and **Bladons** department stores was about to start. After years of negotiation, frustration and delay, they had at last received their building licences.

SEPTEMBER.

12th   Over 500 attended a dedication service led by Rev. A.J. Howitt (District Chairman) to mark the opening by Mrs Amy Hollingsworth of the first phase of **Bricknell Avenue Methodist Church**. The £23,000 building with a 250-seater hall and various classrooms was used for worship until the church proper was built in 1957 when it became the church hall. These were the first new Methodist premises to be completed in Hull since the war.

20th   The biggest AFS exercise the country had yet seen took place in the Town Docks area of Hull when 500 personnel and 70 fire appliances from 15 other Yorkshire towns converged on the city. The idea was to simulate an atom bomb attack as realistically as possible.

Work was about to start on three imposing modern blocks of six-storey flats on a site bounded by Porter Street, St. Luke's Street and Adelaide Street that had once been occupied by unsightly slum housing. J. Mather & Son were to build the 69 flats for £161,000 which on completion in late-1956 would be the highest in the city.

Coronation flags were brought out again and houses across the city decked with bunting to welcome back soldiers from the Korean War. After months of worry and heartache, women cheered and wept with joy as a party of Hull and East Riding men docked at Southampton aboard the *Asturias*. A huge bonfire was lit in Moorhouse Road where nearly a thousand turned out to greet Private Ronald Cook. Sadly eight Hull men are known to have died in the conflict.

OCTOBER.

1st   Six new AEC Regent III double-deck buses went into service with Hull Corporation Transport. They were the last KHCT buses to have open rear platforms but, with their stylish radiator covers, were considered by many to be the most handsome ever purchased.

5th   Workmen began fitting flashing yellow beacons to Hull's 90 zebra crossings to comply with new Government regulations. Five crossings in Jameson Street were the first to be 'switched on', the rest following by the year end. The beacons were timed to flash 40 times a minute by both day and night.

6th   **St. Mark's Church**, Anlaby Common was consecrated by the Archbishop of York, Dr. C. Garbutt, after a major rebuilding scheme had added a tower, two side aisles and choir vestries. Most of the pews were salvaged from blitzed churches and adapted for use by the vicar and church volunteers. The original building dated from 1930.

7th   The Sheriff of Hull opened a temporary library at Francis Askew School to serve the Gipsyville district. The West Hull Tenants Association had requested the facility in the 1920s but first depression and then war had prevented action. A site had been reserved for a permanent building once restrictions were removed.

9th   Lord Strabolgi, the former naval heavyweight boxing champion and Central Hull MP Commander J.M. Kenworthy, died in London. A huge man who completely dominated a stage, he had shocked Hull Liberals in 1926 by defecting to the Labour Party at a railwaymen's meeting in Queens Hall.

15th   A tragedy occurred at the hardware store of S.P. Wood Ltd. in Paragon Street. The assistants had been preparing fireworks for sale when there was a huge flash and the entire stock suddenly went up to the ceiling, filling the shop with smoke and flames. Some of the staff escaped after breaking a plate glass window with a jackplane but others were injured jumping from rear windows on to waste ground. Six people were taken to the Infirmary with burns and shock and one, a director of the firm, later died.

21st   Mr. Basil N. Reckitt opened the new clubroom of **Hull City Police Boys Club** at Elm Avenue, Garden Village, replacing premises in Dansom Lane. The facilities included a large gymnastics room with boxing ring, table tennis and billiards rooms, a library, two handicraft rooms and a canteen.

NOVEMBER.

7th   It was the end of a proud era in Hull as the last nine railway horses left Wakefield Street Stables bound for the railway horse depot in Manchester. British Railways were phasing out their faithful servants apart from two shunt horses to be retained a little longer on the docks. Wakefield Street, with a staff of 30, had been the largest of several Hull railway stables that once housed 800 horses between them. It was a sad day for the men who had known and worked with horses all their lives. When people wrote to the Hull Daily Mail concerned about the horses' fate, British Railways issued an assurance that they were going to good employers or retirement homes and would not be slaughtered.

12th   700 youngsters crowded in to Courtney Street Baptist Church, where the Rev. Harry Whitaker of Middlesbrough and Rev. L.V. Jiggins of Leeds were conducting a high-pressure campaign to bring the Christian message to the district. Film strips, talkies, a bible quiz and rousing choruses were among the attractions on offer.

DECEMBER.

2nd   The newly-built Junior and Infants Departments at **Francis Askew School** were handed over by Councillor R.W. Buckle of the Education Committee to Mr. G. Winters, chairman of the governors. The £150,000 buildings provided 16 classrooms for 800 children plus a nursery for the under fives.

3rd   Hull's importance as a timber importing centre was underlined when merchants Horsley Smith & Co. Ltd. invited trade representatives to inspect their new '**Coronation Shed**' on Victoria Dock. The 440 ft. x 163 ft. timber-built structure was the biggest of its kind in the country, allowing gangs to pile wood on to wagons in all weathers as well as providing dry storage for 2,500 standards. A celebratory luncheon was held at the Royal Station Hotel.

15th   Thick fog blanketed the city during the evening and lines of immobilised buses and cars blocked the roads as visibility dropped to about a yard. Scarves and handkerchiefs became makeshift smog masks and at one stage people were bumping into one another in the streets. The acrid, smoky fog even penetrated houses making the air hazy and causing coughing.

24th   For the second time in two weeks flood water crept up towards houses along a half mile stretch of Hessle High Road when sluice gates jammed near St. Andrew's Dock. Gardens were flooded and the road surface lifted near the construction site of the new trunk sewer. Further along the road a new method of sewer building was being tried for the first time in Hull. Air pressure machinery and a cutting shield were driving a tunnel 30 ft. beneath the road. Work was going on by day and night at a rate of 90-100 ft. a week, far faster than the 'open cut' method used before.

The Hollywood comedy duo Laurel and Hardy appeared at the Palace Theatre during their third and final visit to England.

NUMBER OF VEHICLES LICENSED IN HULL.

September 1953

Private Cars	10,280
Powered bicycles	1,438
Motorcycles	4,856
Goods vehicles	6,168
Ambulances	237
Tractors	287
Pedestrian controlled vehicles (eg. milk trolleys)	6,424
Total	**29,690**

Information: Hull City Council.

Hull's big industrial firms played their part in the Coronation effort by decorating their works with flags and bunting. This impressive banner at Reckitt & Colman Ltd. was an ingenious method of concealing unsightly pipework crossing Dansom Lane! Reckitt's newly-completed office block stands behind. Photograph by courtesy of Reckitt & Colman Products Ltd.

THE QUEEN'S CORONATION.

The Coronation of Her Majesty Queen Elizabeth II took place on Tuesday 2nd June 1953 but almost a year before the great day the City Council formed a Coronation (Special) Committee to make 'fitting arrangements' for its commemoration in Britain's Third Port.

The Committee sought authority to spend the product of a 2d. rate (around £14,000) on their plans which included presenting each of the city's 52,000 schoolchildren with a silver plated spoon and a 2oz. bag of sweets. The spoon handles were engraved with the Queen's head adorned with a crown and the inscription 'Elizabeth R, Coronation 1953' and, on the reverse, the city's three crowns and the words 'Kingston upon Hull'. The children were also treated to two extra half-day holidays besides Coronation Day itself in the week after the Whit break. Every citizen over 70 years of age was to get a sparkling five shilling piece to treasure as a memento of this their fourth coronation.

An amazing catalogue of festivities for people of all ages was planned for Coronation Week. There were to be bands and concert parties in the parks and at the Pier; variety shows, musical revues and firework displays; a Bowls Drive at Costello; a funfair, model yachts, motor boat races and archery contests at East Park; firefighting displays at the Central Fire Station and a children's painting competition.

Impressive though the official plans were it was the way the people themselves, in families or groups, rallied round to organise their own celebrations and enter into the spirit of the occasion that made the 1953 Coronation one of the great events of our time. People spent hours cutting out, sticking, sewing and putting up banners, streamers and bunting until it seemed as if the whole of Hull from the grandest thoroughfare to the humblest terrace had been splashed with red, white and blue paint. Street Committees got busy collecting hundreds of pounds to provide street parties and no fewer than 607 permits were issued in the area covered by Hull Food Office, each party averaging 200-300 guests.

Business and voluntary organisations were equally keen to do their bit. Big firms like Reckitts and the department stores lavishly decorated their buildings and even ships in the docks were gaily trimmed with bunting and flags. Hull Chamber of Trade held a Shopping Festival and issued 20,000 copies of a souvenir handbook. The Hull Daily Mail took 450 people by special express excursion train to London for a preview of the capital city's decorations. Members of the Haworth Evening Townswomen's Guild decided to mark the event in a more lasting way. Early on the morning of 19th May they began planting 2,000 bedding plants, bought with the proceeds of jumble sales, to brighten up the central strip along Beverley High Road!

Hull Parks Department made a special effort for Coronation Year, planting close on 400,000 summer plants in the parks and verges, in tubs and baskets and around the fountain in Queens Gardens, compared with the normal output of 250,000. The city had never looked so colourful and the favourable comments made by citizens and visitors alike were well deserved.

Coronation Day itself was cold and rainy. During the Abbey Service Hull's streets were deserted as, for the first time in history, families, neighbours and friends huddled round television sets to witness the event first-hand. Many of the sets had been hurriedly bought or rented specially for the occasion. Unfortunately the weather was unkind to the street parties, some of which moved indoors while others carried on regardless, the children bravely running around in colourful but scanty costumes. The Sheriff of Hull (Councillor Bertie Svenson) and Deputy Lord Mayor (Councillor J.L. Schultz) and their ladies made a whirlwind tour taking civic greetings to the people and all over the city it seemed nothing could dampen the Coronation spirit of happy togetherness.

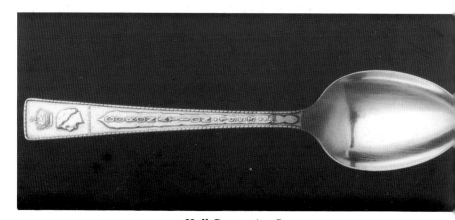

Hull Coronation Spoon.
By courtesy of Mr. A. Ripley.

After years of privation, Coronation Day offered a good excuse for a street party. With certain foodstuffs still rationed, a permit had to be sought from the Food Office. Most groups didn't allow a detail like the weather to wash away their festivities and simply moved indoors like this happy gathering in Brighton Street. Photograph by courtesy of Innes Studios, Hessle.

A scene almost unique in a British city - ships making an appearance in the city centre. The trawler `Thornella` moored in Princes Dock, near to Monument Bridge. Few citizens could resist pausing to watch the dock activity from this spot as they passed between the Old Town and Queen Victoria Square. Photograph by Harry Cartlidge.

1954

The year that:-

Roger Bannister was the first man to run a mile in under four minutes.

The television licence fee was raised from £2 to £3 a year.

All food rationing ended in Britain.

Lester Piggott had his first Derby victory on 'Never Say Die'.

Millions flocked to hear American evangelist Billy Graham who preached for 72 consecutive nights during his British tour.

Kingsley Amis's 'Lucky Jim' and J.R.R. Tolkien's 'Lord of the Rings' were published.

A new Morris Minor cost £440.

JANUARY.

12th   Sir Arthur Hutchinson (Deputy Under Secretary of State for the Home Office Fire Department) accompanied by Mr. H.M. Smith (Chief Inspector of Fire Services) opened the new **Auxiliary Fire Service headquarters** in the former Little Theatre in Kingston Square. The theatre's sloping floor had been levelled to garage 20 green fire appliances and the dressing rooms converted into lecture and recreation rooms and a bar. Pulleys and hoists which once moved the stage scenery were now used to hang fire hoses up to dry. Hull thus became the only place in the North-East to have special headquarters for its 320 AFS volunteers.

19th   The inaugural meeting of the Corporation's War Damaged Sites Committee was held. It was brought into being to arrange the clearance of Hull's many unsightly bombed sites and to plan their short-term conversion into temporary gardens, car parks or children's playgrounds pending more permanent forms of development.

30th   Two steam locomotives hauling the morning express from Kings Cross, due into Paragon Station at 12.53 p.m., shunted into the buffers after failing to stop at the end of platform 5. The waiting room was hurriedly turned into a temporary first aid centre and twenty people were taken to the Infirmary suffering from shock and cuts from broken mirrors.

Two new schools were handed over to their governors by Councillor J.L. Schultz, the Deputy Lord Mayor. **Wivern Road Infants School** became the second school to serve Bilton Grange while the 280-pupil **Appleton Primary School** was opened to relieve overcrowding at Bricknell Avenue. A few days later **Estcourt Primary School** was handed over by Councillor R.W. Buckle after a rebuilding project.

FEBRUARY.

11th   Following the elevation of Mr. Richard Law MP (the son of former Prime Minister Bonar Law) to the peerage as Lord Coleraine, a by-election in the Hull Haltemprice Division returned Major Patrick Wall for the Conservatives. Major Wall cancelled a honeymoon cruise to fight the seat.

22nd   Cinemascope, or wide-screen cinema, had its first showing in Hull when 250 guests including the Lord Mayor and Sheriff and their ladies attended the Dorchester to see 'The Robe' starring Richard Burton and Jean Simmons. The 39 ft. screen was double the normal width giving an effect described as startling, with the actors almost leaping out of the screen and the audience feeling as if they were taking part. The glorious days of cinema were certainly not yet over; after losing four cinemas in the war, Mr. Brinley Evans' Hull Cinema Co. chain was offered a new site on Bilton Grange by the Corporation and it was thought there might be a demand for one on Bricknell Avenue as well.

22nd   A new way of shopping was introduced to the people of North Hull when the Greenwood Avenue grocery branch became the first Hull Co-operative Society store to change over to self-service methods.

27th   The Home Secretary, Sir David Maxwell Fyfe, unveiled a plaque to mark the official opening of the **Imperial Typewriters factory** on Hedon Road. The almost completed £½m. building was designed by Messrs. Priestman & Lazenby and built by Quibell & Son Ltd. Work began in July 1951 and would have been finished a year later but for the steel shortage. Production eventually started on a modest scale in November 1953, a small nucleus of staff being trained by key personnel brought from the firm's Leicester headquarters as the machinery gradually arrived on site. Hull was to specialise in portable typewriters with half the output going for export. The whole building was light and airy and the staff facilities were first-class, with one of the largest canteens in the North (incorporating a stage for shows or dance bands), an open air terrace garden for off-duty relaxation and provision for a sports ground. 23 acres remained for future expansion and there were high hopes that this new industry would have a marked effect on the chronic unemployment problem. Regrettably it was not to be. In 1958 50 Hull jobs were axed and the Leicester factory went on short time owing to lack of orders.

MARCH.

4th A nasty accident occurred on Beverley Road when a crowded early morning no.17 bus from North Hull Estate skidded and rammed into Wm. Cussons' grocery shop after the driver swerved to avoid a fallen cyclist. Crowbars were used to free passengers trapped under the crumpled bus roof and 22 were treated at Hull Royal Infirmary. The shop had to be shored up.

10th The Hull tug *Fenman* turned over and sank in the Humber just off Alexandra Dock while towing the steamer *Rudolf* into port. The tug's master lost his life and two crew members were missing.

22nd Workmen began pulling down the gaunt remains of the old **Cecil Cinema**, a prominent eyesore and reminder of Hull's war wounds at the corner of Anlaby Road and Ferensway, to make way for road improvements. The job, a tricky one because of traffic at the busy junction, was programmed to take 4½ months but was actually completed by Sam Allon Ltd. in just over three weeks, one of the local firm's proudest achievements.

Another landmark being demolished was **Cannon Street Station**. A makeshift wooden affair with an arched roof and two double-faced platforms, it had been the terminus of the Hull & Barnsley Railway. Regular traffic had been modest compared with Hull's main station but in its heyday, before motoring became popular, thousands had passed through to board football specials and excursions to such places as London, Blackpool and Brighton. Since 1924, when all passenger trains were re-routed into Paragon, it had been used as a goods station but now only the coal and mineral sidings remained.

APRIL.

14th The **Thomas Hudson Memorial Homes**, three bungalows in Coltman Street designed by the City Architect for elderly people connected with the fishing industry, were handed over to their occupiers in memory of trawler owner Mr. Tom Hudson senior.

Reconstruction of **No. 12 Quay at King George Dock**, the largest dock improvement scheme for a decade, was finished three months ahead of schedule. The new quarter-mile reinforced concrete quay with high speed cranes and railway lines replaced timber decking and allowed three of the largest ships using the port to berth at once thus speeding up turnround times. The first ship to use the new facility had been the ss. *Luciano* discharging 7,500 tons of Australian sugar in September 1953.

The Works Committee were examining the problems of traffic and pedestrian conflict in Queen Victoria Square, caused by the ever rising tempo of modern traffic in an area never designed for it. The City Engineer described the square, with seven busy converging streets, five zebra crossings and three policemen on point duty, as a 'nightmare'. A census showed that 18,000 pedestrians used the area in a ten-hour period and Hull Accident Prevention Council thought it warranted subways like those in Piccadilly Circus.

MAY.

2nd Mr. Hugh Gaitskell MP (former Chancellor of the Exchequer) addressed a mass meeting in the City Hall after a May Day rally at Corporation Field. Members of the Labour, Co-operative and Trade Union movements, some carrying 'ban the bomb' placards, were led in procession by the Railwaymen's Silver Band.

9th It was a happy day for Hull's Danish community, Prince and Princess Georg of Denmark and His Excellency Steensen-Leth (the new Danish Ambassador) paying a visit to open the **Danish Church** in Osborne Street. The £14,000 contemporary-style building with its separate distinctive bell tower stood across the road from its predecessor, lost in an air raid exactly 13 years earlier. In the meantime services had been held in a wooden church shipped over from Denmark. Hull was the only British city to have three Scandinavian churches.

15th At 12 noon in the Lord Mayor's Parlour an historic announcement was made that the University College had been granted a Royal Charter and become the **University of Hull**. Lord Middleton was to be the first Chancellor and Mr. J.H. Nicholson Vice-Chancellor and it would have the power to confer degrees and honorary degrees in its own right where previously they were granted through the University of London. With the creation of Yorkshire's third and England's 14th university Hull became a University City, thus

Self-service shopping first came to North Hull when the Greenwood Avenue Branch of the Co-op was re-modelled in 1954. The old counters disappeared, merchandise was displayed on low shelves and a pile of baskets greeted customers on the opening day. Photograph by courtesy of Innes Studios, Hessle.

Hull's devastated look lingered well into the 1950s, until funds could be found to either demolish or restore the ruined buildings. The Convent of Mercy and St. Mary's High School, once a prominent feature of Anlaby Road, was finally pulled down in 1954. Photograph by courtesy of Sam Allon Collection.

realising the ideals of its founder Mr. T.R. Ferens. In a flourish of excitement a convoy of undergraduates cycled through the streets to Queens Gardens to celebrate the news. A governing body - the University Court - was formed representing all aspects of Hull life and an appeal for £½m. launched to enable full advantage to be taken of the new status. There were plans to purchase scientific equipment, build a library for a million books, provide a chapel, theatre, gymnasium and swimming pool and set up new academic departments over a ten year period. Since the College was established in 1927 the number of full-time students had already grown to around 800.

17th   Awaiting his entry cue in the wings of the Tivoli Theatre, stage and screen star Arthur Lucan, known to millions as the crochety, eccentric Irish washerwoman Old Mother Riley, suddenly collapsed. Ten minutes later he died of heart failure in the arms of chief electrician, Mr. Roland Watson. In true showbusiness fashion his understudy quickly donned his costume and the show went on. The manager Mr. Harold Clarke broke the news to his widow Kitty McShane in London. Grimsby-born Lucan had played the legendary character for nearly forty years giving pleasure to all ages. He was buried in the Eastern Cemetery after a service at St. Patrick's Church with his stage clothes draped on his coffin.

A new concrete North Stand for 1,500 spectators was opened at **Hull Cricket Club** replacing the one destroyed in the war. Designed by Messrs. Wheatley & Houldsworth and built by Markwell, Holmes and Hayter it included a tea room and bar.

Noise and vibration from tunnelling work on the West Hull main drainage scheme was causing misery day and night for residents in the Brighton Street area. Sixteen houses were so badly affected by subsidence that they eventually had to be evacuated and the residents re-housed on Corporation estates.

Hull's Development Committee, chaired by Alderman Frederick Holmes, suffered a setback with the news that Courtaulds (internationally known manufacturers of artificial silk yarns) had finally lost interest in the old Hedon Road aerodrome site and were to buy land and employ 400 at Grimsby instead. The main reason for their decision was Hull's inadequate water supply (*see page 70*). Negotiations with the firm had been 'on and off' for years, an earlier disappointment coming in May 1952 when a recession in the textile industry forced them to shelve expansion plans.

JUNE.

11th   Government approval was given for a £250,000 four-storey stone and glass building to be erected on the north side of Queens Gardens to house the city's **Police Headquarters**. The existing headquarters in Alfred Gelder Street had been sold to Littlewoods Stores for future expansion and were being leased until the move. When work began early in 1955, the first job was to demolish the network of steel girders put up in the 1930s on adjoining land. This eyesore formed part of an earlier project abandoned when hostilities broke out, the plans for which were now out of date.

29th   A conference involving 16 local authorities from East Yorkshire and North Lincolnshire re-affirmed the need for a **Humber Bridge**. It agreed to ask a London firm of consulting engineers, Freeman, Fox & Partners, to prepare preliminary drawings and specifications to enable a scheme to be put before the Minister of Transport for his consideration. The councils believed a bridge to be of such national importance that it should form part of Britain's trunk road system.

JULY.

1st   An unusual Norwegian exhibition featuring 'Jonah the Giant Whale' was staged on Ferensway Car Park for several days. According to publicity the colossal creature was 66 ft. long, weighed 69 tons and its heart pumped 22,000 gallons of blood every minute!

1st   After a three year wait Hull Corporation heard from the Ministry of Housing & Local Government that their Development Plan had been approved, with only a few minor reservations such as the need for, and alignment of, the proposed intermediate ring road. Many projects that had been held up pending approval could now be progressed.

3rd   Housewives were bracing themselves for big price rises as meat and bacon came off rationing, the last food items to be controlled. Buyers at Hull's Monday Cattle Market eagerly awaited the first 'free' sales for 14 years. Local butchers had prepared for the new market conditions by setting up a non-profit making consortium, Hull Butchers Co. Ltd., to organise joint slaughtering facilities. The city had only three abattoirs compared with 37 before the war and there was concern about the quality of meat brought in from other areas. The Corporation had visions of building a modern central abattoir in Edward's Place but Government spending restrictions thwarted the project.

28th Prompted by the success of those at Bilton Grange and Gipsyville, a 6,000 volume temporary **Branch Library at Bricknell Avenue School** was opened by the Lord Mayor. Another was soon to follow at Sutton.

The general manager of Associated Humber Lines welcomed guests on board the new mv. *Whitby Abbey* at Albert Dock, the first of four replacements for their ageing vessels employed on the near Continental trade.

Ian Carmichael, a 34-year old Hull-born actor, landed a screen part as a British POW in 'The Colditz Story' marking his 'arrival' as a film character actor. After his first success on the London stage in May 1951 in 'The Lyric Revue' he had gone on to become a leading comedian, always at his best playing upper class fools.

BEA announced plans for a helicopter network linking Hull with other British and Continental cities by the early 1960s. They planned to use 150 mph. twin-engine helicopters seating 40-45 passengers. Several sites for a landing pad were looked at including Corporation Field, the Fairground and Anlaby Road Cricket Circle but Sammy's Point emerged as first choice. Paragon Station roof, although most convenient for users, was ruled out because the noise would have disturbed city centre life.

AUGUST.

17th Shipping in the port was paralysed by a strike of 4,000 dockers demanding the abolition of grain discharge by hand. The dispute, similar to that of July 1953, started when 12 Cardiff dockers refused to work the ss. *Seaboard Enterprise* that had been unable to get a silo berth with modern suction gear. By 1 p.m. it had spread to all docks except the Fish Dock and 60 ships lay idle. After an 11 day stoppage the employers agreed to abolish the archaic 'bag filling' system. The dispute did however open up a rift between the dockers and the Transport & General Workers Union. Some of the men 'defected' to the breakaway National Amalgamated Stevedores & Dockers Union (the Blue Union) which, although not recognised by the employers, was keen to recruit and establish itself in the provinces. Relations between the rival unions were the cause of much dockland friction in the years to come.

Another relic of pre-war Hull was disappearing as workmen removed the 'Silver Grill' café, the last building on the site bounded by West Street, Jameson Street and King Edward Street, to make way for another Ravenseft development. Pile driving started on 28th and

it was hoped to complete the project in 12-18 months. There was to be a large Woolworths store and 11 other shops with stock rooms above. Although harmonising with the neo-Georgian style of nearby Queens House the design was more contemporary using rough golden brown bricks, Portland stone dressings and Travertine Marble panelling and ranged from four storeys on the corner down to three at the flanks, where it joined on to Fleet Chambers and Cowleys shoe shop. Loading and car parking would be at the rear.

Improvements completed at **Hull F.C.'s Boulevard ground** included a new East stand and a Supporters Clubroom near the main entrance, opened by Lt. Col. H.P. Robson, Club President.

SEPTEMBER.

4th After two months of showing only Continental films the **Tivoli Theatre** in Paragon Street finally closed its doors. The 875-seat theatre had presented afternoon cinema for some time and this had been extended to evenings after the last live show on 10th July. Over the years most British music hall stars had trodden the boards there and it had been a favourite port of call for generations of Hull trawlermen between trips. The directors were negotiating the sale of the property which would mean the end of more than a century of entertainment on the site.

24th H.R.H. The Princess Royal visited Hull to open a six-floor £200,000 extension at the **Sutton Annexe Hospital** which was henceforth to be known as Hull Royal Infirmary (Sutton). Designed by Mr. Richard Mellor (Leeds Regional Hospital Board architect) and built by Spooners (Hull) Ltd., the development doubled the accommodation for medical and surgical cases and included four floors of wards with 116 beds, a magnificent patients' sun lounge with panoramic views towards Lincolnshire, a flat roof where patients could sit for recuperation and a basement air raid shelter. Owing to a shortage of nurses, the new block was unable to open until October. While in Hull the Princess opened the refurbished **Merchant Navy Hotel** in Anlaby Road which aimed to provide cheerful accommodation and reasonably-priced meals for visiting seamen.

29th The finals of a successful talent competition held in the parks during the summer months took place in the City Hall. 3,400 people had watched 110 acts take part in the heats. Nurturing local talent and noting the best amateur performers was essential for Hull's BBC Top Town entry according to Mr. H. Roscoe, Parks Superintendent. Now there were plans to challenge other Yorkshire

Many older citizens will recall the Silver Grill restaurant that stood near the corner of King Edward Street and Jameson Street. It was swept away to make way for the Fletchers Corner development. Photograph by courtesy of Hull City Record Office.

Houses and maisonettes on the Longhill Estate, illustrating to good effect the deliberate policy of retaining the original mature trees in order to create a 'garden city' environment. Photograph by Harry Cartlidge.

towns on a home and away basis.

There was controversy at the Transport Committee over spending £60,000 on reconstructing the highway in Park Avenue so that the no. 14 buses could continue to run along it.

Great Universal Stores Ltd. acquired a controlling interest in Bladons Ltd., the Hull drapery and furnishing business that had traded in Prospect Street for over 80 years. Existing staff and trading methods were to be retained.

OCTOBER.

9th   Hull Civic and Trades Exhibition was one of the most ambitious events ever staged at the City Hall. It featured demonstrations by Hull's leading industries, examples of civic plate and Trinity House silver, model railway displays and performances by Ceres Harper's Light Orchestra. A 1/12th scale model of the Council Chamber made by students at the Technical College attracted great interest.

14th   A large portion of the older part of the city was flooded when an exceptionally heavy tide caused the River Hull to overflow at 6 a.m. Mytongate and parts of Market Place were badly affected and water was nearly a foot deep in High Street and Blackfriargate. Office workers, street sweepers and housewives were kept busy getting rid of the aftermath. The Lord Mayor promised to call a conference to discuss what could be done to prevent it happening again.

22nd   Hammonds Ltd. became the first city centre store to open a self-service grocery department. It was located in the basement and remained a popular feature for nearly thirty years. For the run up to Christmas a 10,000 sq.ft. extension came into use on the third floor to create the largest Toy Fair in the East Riding, a delight for the city's youngsters.

Now that vacant sites were rapidly being taken up for construction work, Hull would soon face grave car parking problems, according to a report by the Town Planning Officer. Over 1,500 cars were parked in the central area each day, a number that was increasing at an alarming rate. Suggestions for easing the problem included building multi-storey parks and excavating Queens Gardens to make an underground car park.

Public notice was given of the intention to remove the remains of 230 human bodies buried between 1838 and 1854 in the Waltham Street churchyard to make way for the foundations of a new Hull Methodist Mission. They were in the vaults of the old demolished chapel and unless claimed within two months would be cremated at Hedon Road Crematorium. The new mission was being planned as a more central alternative to the existing Queens Hall in Alfred Gelder Street.

Hull Corporation's Finance Committee offered congratulations to Mr. C.H. Pollard on reaching a milestone in his career - his Silver Jubilee as City Treasurer. During that period he had reached great eminence in his profession, the chairman remarked.

Local singer David Whitfield, who had risen to stardom overnight, was among artistes selected for the Royal Variety Performance at the London Palladium.

NOVEMBER.

5th   Hull's first post-war Church of England school, the **Archbishop William Temple School** in Westcott Street, was officially opened by Mr. Dennis Vosper MP (Parliamentary Secretary to the Minister of Education) and dedicated by the Archbishop of York. It filled a gap left by the closure of several church schools over the years and was so named to commemorate the former Archbishop's deep interest in education. Mr. S. Hobson (Chief Education Officer) told 130 newly-appointed teachers that they had come to Hull at a most exciting time in its educational development when it faced the biggest school building programme in history. Twenty new schools had been built since the war and another 16-20 were planned over the next four years. The effects of the post-war 'baby bulge' had hit the primary schools in 1951 and now Hull had more pupils for its size than any other large city apart from Liverpool. The roll had risen from 45,000 in 1945 to 53,000 and was likely to top 59,000 by 1960. The problem was further aggravated by the redistribution of population to the new housing estates and the need to restore war-damaged classrooms. Many schools were seriously overcrowded, some even holding classes in nearby church halls or other hired rooms.

12th   For the second time in less than a month it was a day of misery for many as flood waters poured into the Old Town and Witham area, trapping families in their homes, following the highest tide in living memory. It was the worst flood since 1921, the water reaching 3'4" above expected levels at the Pier. The next day Mr.

Duncan Sandys, Minister of Housing and Local Government, accompanied by MPs, made a 200 mile dash to inspect the havoc. All agreed that the flooding was on a serious scale and those who had suffered showed amazing fortitude. The mopping-up operation - 'Operation Air Dryer'- began over the weekend when the WVS, City Police and RAF personnel took 30 petrol-driven hot air machines around the area on vehicles. The machines were normally used for heating aircraft engines and guns in cold weather. The Lord Mayor launched an appeal fund for the 1,400 distressed families, which raised over £8,600. It was found that the river had overflowed in 31 places prompting the Corporation to consider enforcing a 1925 Act that compelled landowners to build up their banks.

29th   Hull University student, R.G. Hattersley, who in later life was destined to become the Deputy Leader of the Labour Party, took part in the regional final of a Students Union debating tournament. He proposed a motion, 'That in the opinion of this house, conscience is an unmitigated nuisance'.

30th   Hull Food Office, located at Bevin House since the early days of the war and now made redundant by the end of rationing, closed down with the loss of 14 civil service jobs.

There was a heated debate at the Baths Committee over plans to build a new Corporation Wash House in Victor Street. Some members thought they were a thing of the past now that launderettes were opening throughout Hull and a scheme existed for hiring out washers.   Others claimed they provided a convivial meeting place for housewives and the crowd spirit should not be overlooked. The £66,000 scheme was never implemented.

The east side of King Edward Street was coming back to life as the first shops in the **Triangle Development** neared completion. Burtons Tailoring and Stead & Simpsons had already opened and more followed by the new year. The main contractors, Spooners Ltd., had been on site since March.

Two more new schools, **Wold Road Junior** and **Bellfield Primary**, were handed over to their governors by Councillor J.L. Schultz.

DECEMBER

5th   There were numerous grumbles from the travelling public when Hull Corporation Transport introduced their biggest timetable reorganisation for years. Bus frequencies were reduced on several routes in an effort to cut mounting financial losses.

8th   Many West Hull residents were awakened suddenly when two goods trains on the overhead line collided near Tennyson Avenue at 2 a.m. No one was hurt but several 40-ton grain hoppers toppled down the embankment and six wagons were reduced to matchwood.

11th   Hull became the 23rd place in the country to join the Post Office's speaking clock service when Mr. David Gammans (Assistant Postmaster General) made the first '96' call to TIM while opening a Telecommunications Exhibition at the Mortimer Gallery.   The reply - 2.56 p.m. and 20 seconds - was relayed across Victoria Square by loud hailer.   The exhibition celebrated the Golden Jubilee of the city's municipal telephone system which now had 45,000 subscribers.   Mr. Gammans praised the unique undertaking which was still offering 2d. local calls - a penny cheaper than the GPO - and was world famous for its Father Christmas link-up. To mark the Jubilee the classified section of the 1954 Hull telephone directory was printed for the first time on golden pages (later referred to as 'yellow pages'). The Post Office followed suit in 1965 since when the practice has been adopted almost universally by classified trade publications.

13th   There was a big pre-dawn blaze at Hull coconut flour millers, Clark & Letham Ltd.'s four-storey premises in Pryme Street causing £30,000 worth of damage.

A temporary church inside the blitzed shell of Christ Church, John Street, ceased to be used as a place of worship and services were transferred to the Charterhouse Chapel.

CHEAP DAY RETURNS FROM HULL BY RAIL		
Summer 1954.		
Bridlington	5/-	(25p)
Filey	6/6	(33p)
Flamborough	5/3	(28p)
Hornsea	2/6	(13p)
Leeds	9/4	(47p)
Scarborough	8/-	(40p)
Withernsea	2/6	(13p)
York	8/-	(40p)
Newcastle (Races)	14/3	(73p)
Manchester	11/-	(55p)

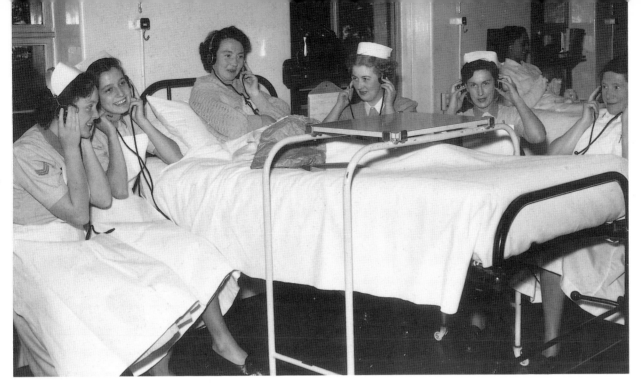

A 116-bed extension to the Sutton Annexe Hospital brought the latest ideas in health care into the Hull area. Nurses gather round a patient's bed to try out the new radio receivers designed to improve patient comfort. Photograph by courtesy of Innes Studios, Hessle.

David Whitfield entertaining at the Palace Theatre. Formerly a builder's labourer, the Hull-born recording artist's first chart topper was 'Answer Me' in 1953. Two years later he was awarded a Golden Disc for selling one million copies of 'Cara Mia'. Photograph by courtesy of Innes Studios, Hessle.

BEATING THE DROUGHT.

One of the biggest problems the Hull authorities had to contend with in the 'fifties concerned the city's water supply.

The Hull Corporation Water Department served about 400,000 people in a 312 square mile area extending from Hornsea to Brough. Supply was derived entirely from underground sources, being extracted at pumping stations at Springhead, Cottingham and Dunswell from wells connected to an underground network of 'adits' penetrating deep into the chalk strata of the Yorkshire Wolds. Since it took four months for rain falling on the Wolds to reach the tap a good winter rainfall was essential to allow adequate stocks to build up in the reservoirs to meet peak summer demand.

As early as 1947 there were signs of a shortage developing but by the summer of 1953 the effect of two consecutive dry winters had caused it to reach critical proportions. The position continued to deteriorate and by Christmas the pumping stations could only manage to produce 14.1 million gallons a day against a daily demand of 17.75 millions. Already mains pressure had been reduced at certain times of day affecting trade and domestic consumers alike. Industrial processes that relied on water, such as cooling systems, were badly disrupted and several city centre office blocks had no water on the top floor for tea breaks. Fire fighting operations were hindered and there was fear of contamination should impurities find their way into the impoverished pipes. To urge users to economise a desperate plea was made in the Hull Daily Mail: 'WATER SHORTAGE - SUPPLIES ARE DANGEROUSLY LOW - DRASTIC ECONOMY IS ESSENTIAL TO PREVENT FAILURE OF SUPPLY.'

With winter rainfall at only 50% of average the 'drought' continued into the early months of 1954, the third and worst year so far. The crisis threatened the very industrial prosperity of the city and port and members of the Chamber of Commerce and Shipping were deeply concerned. The Development Committee too were dismayed when one after another firms that had shown interest in coming to Hull changed their mind when they learnt that a water supply could not be guaranteed. Batchelors Peas Ltd., the vegetable canners, had planned to bring 1,000 new jobs to the city but called off their proposals in February 1954 when it was clear their requirements for three million gallons a week by 1956 could not be met. Then in May Courtaulds decided to develop at Grimsby rather than Hull for a similar reason. According to a University College survey water was the factor most frequently mentioned when firms were asked why they did not locate in Hull.

Clearly the Corporation had to take urgent action. Powers had been obtained in 1933 to build a reservoir and impound the waters of the Farndale valley in North Yorkshire but the scheme had been deferred owing to the war and was now out of the question on grounds of cost. So to increase supplies in the short term the Water Engineer prepared a cheaper scheme to abstract 12 million gallons a day from the upper reaches of the River Hull, at Hempholme and West Beck, near Driffield. For an outlay of £2.4m. this would meet the current shortfall and provide a daily surplus of eight million gallons.

In October following a public inquiry the Lord Mayor was able to announce that the Minister had given the scheme his blessing, thus securing the city's water supply for the next 15-20 years. Work began in May 1956, the first task being to lay a 36" diameter pipeline from Hempholme to the city boundary at Sutton Road, a distance of 10½ miles. Construction of the river intakes, two storage reservoirs of 280 acres, filtration and pumping plant, and housing for the employees also got under way.

Water was pumped from the Tophill Low Pumping Station as it was named, for the first time on 3rd July, 1959 and though rainfall that year was well below average and demand reached record levels (24.5 million gallons being registered only five days after the station was commissioned) the supply to consumers in Hull and district was maintained without further problems.

Water, water everywhere... but not a drop to drink! The Minister of Housing and Local Government, Mr. Duncan Sandys MP, guides a Hull housewife over sandbags in the Wincolmlee area after floods had wreaked havoc in over a thousand homes. Ironically, the city had recently been suffering from a water shortage. Photograph by courtesy of Innes Studios, Hessle.

Hull's low-lying ground was always liable to flood, especially when heavy rain coincided with high tides. Scenes like this were common at Chanterlands Avenue bridge until the new North Hull trunk sewer intercepted the storm water flow. Photograph by courtesy of Innes Studios, Hessle.

Prospect Street early in 1955. The steelwork being erected formed part of the Woolworth's store while the workmen in front were re-aligning the junction with West Street. The old Hull Royal Infirmary can be seen in the background. Photograph by courtesy of Sam Allon Collection.

1955

The year that:-

Sir Anthony Eden succeeded Churchill as Prime Minister.

The Eastern European countries, including Russia, signed the Warsaw Pact.

The Independent Television Service opened in the London area.

Mr. Attlee retired; Hugh Gaitskell was elected leader of the Parliamentary Labour Party.

Ruth Ellis was the last woman to be executed for murder.

Scientist Dr. Albert Einstein died.

Fish fingers and Wimpy Bars heralded new British eating habits.

JANUARY.

26th   The year opened in a tragic way for Hull's fishing community with the disappearance of two trawlers, the *Lorella* (H455) and *Roderigo* (H135), each with a 20 man crew. After steaming together towards safety in treacherous weather conditions near Iceland's North Cape the vessels had turned back to help another boat stricken with propeller trouble. Falling victim to the notorious 'black frost' which affects this part of the Arctic, first the *Lorella* keeled over and then an hour or so later the *Roderigo*. Despite an exhaustive search by aircraft and shipping no survivors could be traced. A Court of Inquiry later concluded that the trawlers 'capsized and foundered due to an unusual and unpredictable combination of heavy gales, high seas and loss of stability caused by heavy accumulations of ice on their upper structures.'

31st   The final curtain came down on the Janus Theatre after five years of lively endeavour during which the playgoers of Hull shared many glimpses of the greatness of theatre. Like many other companies it had been affected by strong competition from television and this, together with greatly increased rental and running costs, made a second leasehold term impossible. "Prompter" of the Hull Daily Mail in his final tribute to the co-directors Stella Sizer-Simpson and Peter S. Harvey said that the Janus Theatre had been the most courageous theatrical experiment in many years and that it had fulfilled a noble mission.

Thirty-seven people took up residence when **Bilton House**, a new Corporation old people's home opened its doors in Wivern Road. The £29,000 Kingston Home was the second of five authorised in 1949 as part of a plan to end the days of the workhouse, once the only haven of refuge for the elderly. Sixty women at the Beverley Road Hostel and 81 men at the Anlaby Road Hostel were waiting for places in the new homes.

FEBRUARY.

21st   Local grocery chain Wm. Cussons Ltd. were advertising an offer to serve 'all their old age pensioner friends' with their entire food requirements at a discount of 12½% or 2/6d. in the £.

The **New Grafton Hotel** was the name given to the latest public house to open in Hull. Moors & Robsons brewery had been allocated the Grafton Street site, once occupied by a preparatory school, by the Licensing Planning Committee to replace that of the blitzed 'Greenland Fishery' in Cleveland Street which was needed for the expansion of Spillers' flour mills.

MARCH.

12th   The Archbishop of York consecrated the newly-completed **St. Aidan's Church** in Southcoates Avenue, a simple brick structure designed by Messrs. W. Milner and R.B. Craze. Previously a district church, it now served a parish of its own.

13th   The first buses began operating along Holderness Road to the rapidly-growing Longhill Estate. Although entirely within the city boundary the new route no. 56 was worked by East Yorkshire buses to balance up the mileage factor under the terms of a Co-ordination Agreement between Hull's two main bus operators, KHCT and EYMS. Since 1934 they had been required to share both mileage and fare revenue over a large part of the city.

14th   Sir Brian Robertson (Chairman of the British Transport Commission) made an announcement long awaited by Hull's business community that the Riverside Quay would be rebuilt and brought back into operation. The £1.5 million scheme depended on negotiations with Hull Chamber of Commerce & Shipping, who had pressed for it for many years, and on talks with Hull Corporation about the future of the public right of way along the riverfront. It was hoped the quay would relieve pressure on King George and

Alexandra Docks and give easier access to both Humber Street and the inland markets for perishable produce from the near Continental ports. However there were some doubts that trade would ever return to pre-war dimensions as many Dutch growers who once traded through the port had now set up in Britain.

26th Residents of Pickering Road whose homes backed on to Kingston School fields woke up to find their gardens submerged under 3 ft. of water after nearby drains overflowed. Angry householders pleaded with the Corporation to do something about the area's inadequate drainage.

The Hull drapery store, Willis Bros. Ltd. of Carr Lane, was acquired by Hurst & Sandler Ltd. of Leeds following the death of the governing director Mr. A.H. Willis.

Hull's Health Department took delivery of two new motor ambulances which were noticeably different from earlier examples in the 20-strong fleet. Instead of the usual black and white, a metalescent blue colour scheme was introduced which became standard for Hull ambulances for the next 20 years. For added comfort a new type of stretcher was fitted together with foam beds and more modern heating. These were also the first amb:lances in England to display road safety slogans (such as Drive Safely; Drive with Care), an idea of Dr. A. Hutchison, Medical Officer of Health.

Retail newsagents and booksellers, W.H. Smith Ltd., acquired their first Hull store when they took over Bromby's Ltd. of 3 Monument Buildings, Queen Victoria Square. Bromby's, whose printing and stationery business in Bond Street was unaffected by the change, had been on the site for 60 years. Smith's later moved into the King Edward Street wing of Queens House.

Mr. Alston (Town Planning Officer) considered Hull needed a central trading estate rather like that at Team Valley in order to attract new industries. He suggested that a 213 acre site between Sutton Road, Leads Road and the River Hull could provide up to 6,000 jobs and would be very accessible for workers coming from all parts of the city. At present firms wanting a large site had little choice but to go to Hedon Road or Saltend. However the cost of laying out the area and providing a new main road and drainage would be high.

APRIL.

12th The Asbestos & Rubber Company opened what was claimed to be the best-equipped sports shop in the North of England - **'Asbestos Corner'** - replacing temporary premises nearby in Savile Street. The event marked the completion of another phase of the Triangle Trust scheme and greatly enhanced the approach to the city centre from the east which had been scarred by the destruction of Costello's corner.

16th At 1.55 p.m. Councillor R.E. Tennyson (Chairman of the Telephones Committee) pulled a switch to change over 3,000 lines and open the **North Hull Automatic Telephone Exchange** in Endike Lane. The £175,000 building was intended to relieve pressure on the 1922 Newland Rotary exchange and bring a service to those on the ever-growing waiting list for phones. As part of a far-reaching modernisation programme there were plans to open another exchange at Bilton Bar in the autumn and to convert the manual exchanges at Beverley, Ferriby and Brough to automatic working, a move which meant phasing out the 'hello girls' whose job it was to ask 'number, please' when routeing trunk calls through to Hull Post Office. Local telephone users had just begun to notice a change in Hull's distinctive telephone sounds, bringing them into line with the rest of Britain - the high pitched dialling tone had given way to the GPO's 'sophisticated purr' and Hull's dull click-click ringing tone had been discarded for the more usual 'burr burr'.

Local builder Mr. Stan Spruit was developing a small private housing estate on the city boundary near First Lane, Hessle. Two types of 3 bedroom houses, designed by Roper Spencer & Hall, were on offer in Mollison and Ulverston Roads at prices ranging from £1,690 to £1,785. Rates were 6/4d. a week. There were two show houses furnished by Hammonds of Hull.

MAY.

18th The Bishop of Hull dedicated the new sanctuary chancel, clock and bell turret of **St. George's Church, Marfleet Lane**. These recent additions to what had been a rather nondescript dual-purpose building gave it an unmistakable churchlike appearance and the bell tower contained one of East Hull's few striking clocks.

20th Ben Lyon, with his son Richard and daughter Barbara (the Lyon family of radio, TV, stage and screen fame), visited Hull to open **Phillips Complete Furnishing Store** in the Triangle block in King Edward Street. Nearby **Boots the Chemists** were advertising

A prominent corner in the city centre was greatly enhanced by the completion of the 'Asbestos' sports and leisure shop, another phase of the unique Triangle Trust development. Photograph by courtesy of Hull City Council Department of Planning and Design.

Private housebuilding tended to be in small pockets here and there rather than on the mass scale of the 1930s. These three-bedroom houses in Mollison Road were on the market from £1,690 when new in 1955. Photograph by courtesy of Hull City Council Department of Planning and Design.

the opening of a modern pharmacy (to which their subscription library was transferred from Whitefriargate). **Alexandre** the tailors were also in business on the Savile Street corner.

26th The General Election was fought on new constituency boundaries. Hull Central division had been extinguished and new larger divisions of Hull North and Hull East created. Hull West replaced Hull Haltemprice which had formerly embraced certain areas outside the city. At lunchtime the next day crowds gathered outside the City Hall to hear the results:

Hull East - Cmdr. Harry Pursey (Labour) - majority 12,706.
Hull North - W.R.Austen Hudson (Conservative) - majority 590.
Hull West - Capt. Mark Hewitson (Labour) - majority 5,523.

The **Chamberlain Homes**, 12 new almshouses in Church Street, Sutton provided by the Leonard Chamberlain Charity at a cost of £13,000, were opened. They replaced some older houses dating from 1804.

Spillers Ltd. invited the Lord Mayor and 120 guests to tour their **Swan Mills** in Cleveland Street. The new building had cost over £1 million and been in production for 18 months although only just completed. Its silo could suck in 80 tons of grain an hour from craft on the River Hull and store up to 12,000 tons. Standing 106 ft. high, the mill itself was a landmark for miles around and was capable of processing six tons of wheat every hour to make Spillers' celebrated Turog and Albatross flours.

JUNE.

16th Hull's 'Blue Union' dockers, on strike since 23rd May in a fight to gain recognition for NASDU as a negotiating body, paraded through the streets from King George Dock to Corporation Field where they had been meeting daily. Although there was a police presence the event was amicable, the men marching to music behind banners and the Union Jack, and they enlisted much public sympathy. The dispute, affecting several British ports, ended with a mass return to work on 4th July. Many of the men had lost all their holiday savings.

21st Traders at the west end of Paragon Street heaved a sigh of relief when the road reopened after weeks of diversions, dust and noise caused by reconstruction work. Shopkeepers' representatives had expressed their anger forcefully at Council meetings.

Lt.Col. Rupert Alec-Smith, a keen local historian whose grandfathers founded the timber importing firm Horsley Smith & Co., was appointed leader of the opposition Municipal Association Group on Hull City Council. He succeeded Alderman Cyril Townsley who retired after 19 years.

The end came for Hull's pigfood waste collection drive, a relic of wartime shortages. The scheme began in 1940 when every scrap of waste food for pigs was a contribution to victory. Over 3,000 householders were issued with lidded bins to enable scraps to be collected by Cleansing Department sweepers. The waste had been processed at the Scarborough Street depot and sold as pig and poultry feed but there was no longer a ready market.

The final service was held in the large hall at **Hawthorn Avenue (Norman Memorial) Methodist Church**, the only part to be salvaged after the church suffered extensive damage in the war. In the congregation were several people who had attended the opening services 50 years before. During the summer the building fell under the demolition men's hammers, along with three of Hull's other ruined churches: **St. Thomas's, Campbell Street**; **St. Stephen's**, near the city centre, and **St. Peter's, Drypool**. St. Stephen's, built in 1844 to the designs of H.F. Lockwood, was one of the city's finest Victorian buildings. Its tall spire was a familiar sight to visitors arriving in Hull by train who would set their watches by its clock. The congregation was united with St. Jude's, Spring Bank. At St. Peter's the tower and clock faces, prominent features of the Victoria Dock estate, were retained until 1959.

JULY.

6th Work began on a major project that would greatly benefit North Hull in years to come. The £800,000 contract for the northern arm of the **West Hull and Haltemprice Main Drainage Scheme** involved building a trunk sewer from Walton Street fairground via West Park and Boulevard to the pumping station under construction in West Dock Avenue. One of the first operations was to dig a 30 ft. hole near the cricket ground from where tunnels would be bored in each direction. Starting in the late summer of 1957 the scheme was extended through to Bricknell Avenue and North Hull estate to allow housebuilding to re-commence in these areas (*see page 115*).

19th A scene of splendour was created in the City Hall when representatives of 60 Commonwealth and Continental seats of learning joined with civic heads from 12 Yorkshire towns and cities to congratulate Hull on its elevation from University College to full

Hull Corporation tried out adventure playgrounds as a way of rejuvenating bombed sites and keeping the youngsters off the increasingly busy streets. This de-capitated trolleybus, jacked up on concrete, proved a great attraction at the Linnaeus Street playground. Photograph by courtesy of Kingston upon Hull City Transport Ltd.

Dockers marching through the streets to enlist support for the 'Blue Union' (N.A.S.D.U.) in its fight to gain recognition by the port employers in the summer of 1955. The men had become discontented with the Transport and General Workers Union over its handling of their grievances in the notorious 'bag filling dispute'. Photograph by courtesy of Innes Studios, Hessle.

The first of the floating suction elevators discharging grain from ship to craft in King George Dock. The elevators were brought in to speed up turnround times and avoid 'hand-scuttling'. Photograph by courtesy of Innes Studios, Hessle.

Bilton Grange was Hull's first attempt at 'neighbourhood planning' with the shops and other amenities placed in a market square at the heart of the development rather than along the main roads, where they might invite accidents. Photograph by courtesy of Innes Studios, Hessle.

University status. Lord Middleton was installed as the first Chancellor and honorary degrees were conferred on H.R.H. The Princess Royal, Sir David Hughes Parry, Dr. Arthur Morgan (the College's first Principal) and others. Since the granting of the charter, applications for admission had doubled. Lord Middleton pledged that the University would pursue a policy of expansion but with the emphasis always on quality.

30th Hull's first **Adventure Playground**, in Linnaeus Street, opened as a 12-month experiment. It was an initiative of the War Damaged Sites Committee inspired by the success of similar ventures in America, Scandinavia and England. Instead of the usual swings and roundabouts affair children were encouraged to play creatively, under the watchful eye of a play-leader, by the provision of old timber and bricks, tree logs, commando netting and sand pits. The Committee, having worked with voluntary groups to produce the scheme, promised to open similar playgrounds in other areas if it was a success. The venture was seen as a cost-effective way of giving youngsters endless fun.

30th Steam locomotive No. 67337 hauled the final passenger train between Hull and South Howden after British Railways obtained consent to close the service, said to be losing £350 a week. Two of the nine stations were closed entirely and the others retained for freight and parcels only. East Yorkshire buses were to be duplicated as required. The closure plans caused one of the loudest public outcries ever known in the East Riding village communities with workers and schoolchildren protesting over the extra travelling times. It was claimed the bus from Hull took 24 minutes to reach Willerby and an hour to Little Weighton compared with 12 and 20 minutes respectively by train.

For the 14th consecutive quarter Hull topped the list of large cities, with average savings per head of 14/1d. Over a fifth of the population were now savers, Hull & District Local Savings Committee heard. There were 20,418 members of workplace savings groups, a record 40,300 savers in schools and 5,610 members of street groups.

AUGUST.

2nd After trading in Anne Street for 80 years a compulsory purchase order forced Phillips the Jewellers to move into alternative premises at 16/17 Savile Street.

2nd There was a big afternoon blaze at Thos. Holmes & Sons Ltd.'s tannery in Wincolmlee. Flames were observed leaping 100 ft. into the air and £10,000 worth of damage was caused.

25th The BBC put Hull on the broadcasting map by opening a studio on the top floor of the Guildhall. A short programme was presented on the Home Service in which Michael Barton of Cottingham reviewed Hull's unique telephone service and local journalist James Goodrick told of plans for the level crossings. The studio was to be used for news, short talks and sports reports.

A report and plans of the proposed **Humber Bridge** project, prepared by Sir Gilbert Roberts FRS of Freeman, Fox & Partners of London, arrived in the city. It was on the strength of these that the Humber Bridge Act was passed in 1959. A 4,500 ft. long single-span bridge crossing the Humber at its narrowest point between Hessle and Barton and costing £13 millions was envisaged in seven to eight years time (The actual completion date was 1981).

East Park Gala, a joint Corporation and Sailors Children's Society event, drew 20,000 visitors and was regarded as the best for several years. As an experiment a flower, fruit and vegetable show was organised in a large marquee by Hull & E.R. Allotment Council attracting 180 entries. The Parks Committee hoped it would be the forerunner of a leading annual event for the North-East which would in due course compare with such well-known shows as Southport and Shrewsbury.

Sloane's Billiard Hall in Jameson Street, where many a young man had whiled away the hours in pre-war days and witnessed battles of the giants including the famous Lindrum, was being pulled down to make way for further Triangle Trust buildings.

SEPTEMBER.

1st Rabbi Dr. Meyer Law was in Hull for the consecration of the **Old Hebrew Congregation's Synagogue** at the corner of Anne Street and Osborne Street after reconstruction work costing £27,000. The opening was performed by Mr. L. Rapstone.

2nd Rebuilding of **Hull Co-operative Society's Central Premises**, the last major rehabilitation scheme for Hull's blitzed department stores, got under way. It was to be carried out in phases starting at the back while business continued in a single-storey 'prefab' along the Jameson Street frontage. When finished it would embrace a store, offices, restaurant and dance hall and be the biggest

A proud moment in the life of a city as Lord Middleton is installed as the first Chancellor of the new University of Hull at a special ceremony in the City Hall. One of the recipients of an Honorary Degree was Her Royal Highness The Princess Royal (seated extreme left) who always followed happenings in Hull with great interest. Photograph by courtesy of the University of Hull.

Shoppers squeeze by to grab a bargain at the newly-opened Littlewoods Variety Store in Whitefriargate. With a total counter length of 852 feet, there was no shortage of choice. Photograph by courtesy of Innes Studios, Hessle.

Mr. Robert Greenwood Tarran, master builder, who died in 1955. Photograph from 'Tarranotes' by courtesy of Mr. Maurice Tarran.

building of its kind in the city, enclosing 2.84 million cu.ft. and reaching a height of 85 ft. at the top of its copper dome. The Town Planning Committee praised the 'courageous, handsome design' for attempting to break the city's monotonous skyline.

10th Lord Middleton (President of the East Riding Territorial & Auxiliary Forces Association) officially opened the **Middleton Barracks**, new Territorial Army quarters on Calvert Lane. Designed by Messrs. Priestman & Lazenby and built by Markwell, Holmes & Hayter, they were the first new barracks in Hull since 1914 and accommodated 300 men previously based at Park Street Artillery Barracks and the Albemarle Rooms on Anlaby Road. Special features included a large drill hall/dance floor, a miniature rifle range and parachute training facilities.

13th Alderman Isaac Robinson (Housing Committee Chairman) presided when the Lord Mayor opened the **Bilton Grange Shopping Centre** in Greenwich Avenue. The long-awaited centre, at the heart of Hull's largest post-war housing development, comprised 18 shops with maisonettes around three sides of a quadrangle, linked by a protective canopy. There was room to park a car, leave a bike, push a pram or stand and chat, with the whole area taking on the character of a small-town market square. Apart from two privately-built supermarkets the shops were erected for the Corporation by Scruton & Co. Ltd. and each allocated to a different trade so that all essential needs were catered for. There were plans for a community hall, cinema, public house, health centre, library and swimming bath to create a true focal point for the 8-10,000 strong community.

20th One of Hull's famous sons, Mr. Bob Tarran, died at the age of 63. His name was renowned throughout the world of building for drive and innovation. In pre-war days he was a pioneer of non-conventional houses and noted for the rapid 22-week completion of the Regal cinema; moving the Wilberforce monument as a gift to the city; building Shell House and Electricity House in Ferensway and the Quarry Hill flats in Leeds. In 1931 he had founded the Hull Guild of Building. He became Hull's Chief Air Raid Warden and afterwards Tarran was a household word for prefabs. The funeral service at St. John's Newland, preceded by a cortege through the streets of his home city, was one of the biggest ever seen locally. Another sad loss was that of Lord Calverley (78) who as George Muff had been Labour MP for Hull East from 1929 to 1931 and 1935 to 45.

30th Towed by three tugs, the first of two floating grain elevators arrived at King George Dock from Goole. Capable of moving 200 tons an hour by pneumatic suction over the side of a ship into lighters, the elevators were introduced to speed up grain discharge and relieve congestion at the silo berths following the abolition of hand scuttling after two dockers' strikes.

OCTOBER.

12th The last two railway horses left Hull after being made redundant from Alexandra Dock where they had been used for shunting timber trucks. They were bound for Birmingham and retirement.

19th Five passengers suffered minor injuries and the leading bogies of engine no. 42553 were twisted when the 1 p.m. train from Wakefield rammed the platform-end buffers through the barber's shop wall at Paragon Station. The barbers were startled but unharmed and carried on cutting hair surrounded by broken glass and plaster.

23rd Hull's oldest cinema, the Princes Hall in George Street, changed hands. Miss Marjorie and Mr. Robert Morton (grandchildren of Wm. Morton who built up a local entertainments empire over 40 years) handed over to businessmen Norman Shenker and Maurice Kirman who planned to have the building refurbished and opened under a new name - the Curzon - on Boxing Day. Like its London namesake it was to show mainly Continental films.

27th The **Frank Finn Homes of Rest**, 12 elderly persons' bungalows on the Lodge Street housing estate, were opened. They were designed by the City Architect and built with money left by a prominent Roman Catholic businessman and former Lord Mayor who died in 1940.

Two new stores to open in the city centre were the **Comet electrical showrooms** in George Street (designed by W. Gregory Wilson and built by Quibell & Son Ltd.) and **Segals drapery store** in Chapel Street. At Marfleet the rebuilding of the **Crown Hotel** ('Red L' to its regulars) was also completed. After it was bombed and burnt to the ground in 1941 drinkers had been catered for in makeshift huts.

NOVEMBER.

1st   The Bishop of Hull (Rev. H.T. Vodden) launched a Humberside Church Building Appeal with the object of raising £98,000 to allow the Church of England to expand into the new housing areas. Eight new buildings or extensions were envisaged, starting with St. Thomas (Hotham Road) and followed by Longhill Estate, Sutton Ings, Willerby, Bricknell Avenue and North-East Hull.

11th   After two years of re-construction work **Thornton Varley's** were able to open the first phase of their department store in Brook Street. Designed by Mr. J.W. Beaumont, a leading Manchester store architect, the £400,000 building had three sales floors linked by a staircase lined with fine Italian marble. The first floor was devoted to fashions, introducing the 'shop within a shop' concept, and boasted over 50 fitting rooms. Other features were a food hall and top-floor coffee room and restaurant. Opening offers included 'luxurious fox collar coats' 24 gns; floral pattern Axminster carpets 34/11 a yard and Candlewick bedspreads 45/11. A special turkey luncheon was served to customers on the opening day for 7/6.

13th   The Greatfield bus service was introduced, initially to Ecclesfield Avenue.

25th   Another chain store to open in Hull was **Littlewoods** on a site in Whitefriargate once occupied by the Bank of England. In line with modern trends the counters were laid out to facilitate self-selection by customers. F. Hall & Sons Ltd. were the main contractors. With visions of expansion Littlewoods had bought the adjacent police station in Alfred Gelder Street but the plans did not materialise for 25 years.

28th   Mr. John Davis (managing director of the J. Arthur Rank Organisation) and his wife, film star Dinah Sheridan, declared open the new **Cecil Cinema**. There was a fanfare of trumpets as a tape across the proscenium was cut and director Mr. Brinley Evans fulfilled a vow made when he saw the old Cecil burning that one day it would be rebuilt. The new Cecil was across the road from its predecessor on land occupied by 'the Ship' Trinity House Rest Homes until they too were blitzed. It was the first cinema in England to be completed on a new site since the war and was ready in a remarkably short time, the foundation stone having been laid on 28th April. The £270,000 building, designed by Messrs. Gelder & Kitchen (and winning them an R.I.B.A. Bronze Medal for exceptional merit) was erected by Spooners Ltd. and seated 2,052. It boasted many special features including the largest screen in the country, all the latest stereoscopic sound, a wonderful organ and a large crush hall to minimise queueing in the rain. The Cecil Orchestra played daily in the theatre and café. Although it was a great night for the cinema industry the future was now looking less than rosy. It was estimated that every other house in Hull was now equipped with a television set.

DECEMBER.

23rd   Nine crewmen and a pilot were lost when the Hull trawler *Prince Charles* (H249) ran aground in a snowstorm off the Norwegian coast. The trawler was later brought back to Hull and restored for further duty as the *Loch Melfort*.

The Watch Committee approved the establishment of a police dog section in the Hull City Police force. Two dogs were to be bought initially, building up later to ten, to be used for deterrent effect.

Pressure exerted by Hull business people resulted in British Railways retiming their Paragon to Kings Cross winter service to give the city its fastest ever train connection with the capital - 3 hours 46 minutes. However in 1956 Chamber of Commerce members were still dissatisfied with the morning service - the 7.05 a.m. from Hull didn't reach London until 12.55 p.m. and entailed changing trains at Selby and Doncaster!

The British Transport Commission announced further investment in the port of Hull, making a bid to regain its traditional status as 'Britain's Third and Cheapest Port'. There was to be a new Saltend jetty to provide an extra berth for discharging ocean going tankers and a two-year scheme to repair war damage to No. 1 Fish Quay at St. Andrews Dock, costing £170,000.

The Anlaby Road (Boulevard) level crossing gates reopening to traffic after the passage of a train. Photograph by courtesy of Hull City Record Office.

HULL'S NOTORIOUS LEVEL CROSSINGS.

A constant source of grumbles during the 'fifties was the delay experienced by drivers, bus passengers and cyclists at the numerous level crossings that straddled the city's main radial roads. It was estimated that time spent waiting at the six busiest crossings cost the community £150,000 a year. One route - Spring Bank West - had no fewer than three of these bottlenecks in the space of a mile, leading to almost intolerable congestion at peak periods.

The existence of so many crossings was a product of Hull's peculiar geography which placed its principal docks and its hinterland at opposite sides, its absolutely flat terrain and an intensive, perhaps over exuberant, period of railway building between the years 1840 and 1870. Fortunately in 1885 the promoters of the last local line to be built - the Hull & Barnsley - had the foresight to avoid aggravating the problem by opting for a high level route carried around the city on an embankment.

Level crossings affected Hull life in many ways and over the years the subject became a favourite hobby-horse for after dinner speakers. "Please sir, it's the gates!" was the standard excuse of many a schoolboy berated by his teacher for lateness. The frequent gate closures played havoc with the efforts of bus operators to maintain reliable services. Although the trolleybuses were spaced at 2-5 minute intervals in the timetable, often after a long wait they would arrive in convoy, much to the puzzlement and irritation of intending passengers. No fewer than eleven crossings and five tidal bridges lay athwart KHCT routes.

The problem was highlighted in August 1955 when a serious fire occurred at Thos. Holmes' tannery. It was reported that fire engines had been held up for a minute to allow a train to pass over Wincolmlee within sight of the blazing building. Even though the brigade's 'double-cover' system had coped with the situation it added ammunition to the critics calling for a swift end to this local bugbear. The business community, represented by the Chamber of Commerce & Shipping, was particularly vociferous in this regard and by petition and deputation repeatedly pressed the Corporation to act.

It was not that the authorities were oblivious to the crippling effect of the crossings on trade and industry; schemes for their removal had abounded in the past 50 years. Such plans generally involved combinations of building viaducts, sinking highways in deep subways and laying new branch lines or curves to divert trains to the high-level ring. The problem was getting all parties concerned to agree on a solution and having done so securing the necessary funds. Moreover Hull's unstable subsoil appeared to rule out subways while only 'road-over-rail' schemes (flyovers) qualified for Government grant aid.

With the preparation of the city's post-war Development Plan the opportunity was taken to formulate specific proposals to abandon five crossings by building flyovers and a further five by diverting two sections of track. Of the 16 crossings then in existence the worst were judged to be Anlaby Road (Boulevard) and Hessle Road (Dairycoates). Town Planning surveys showed that on a typical day the Boulevard gates were closed for a total of 3 hours 40 minutes. But at Hessle Road, where road traffic was slightly lighter, they closed no fewer than 130 times, for a total of 6½ hours. The Town Planning Committee decided on balance that Hessle Road should be given priority.

Plans drawn up by the City Engineer were approved early in 1956 and a deputation visited the Ministry of Transport the following year to urge Government sanction. Initially the Ministry favoured tackling Anlaby Road first on account of its heavier vehicle flow and 25% lower cost. However, after protracted negotiations, the Minister conceded in October 1958 and agreed in due course to grant aid the Dairycoates scheme.

A new decade had dawned when work finally got under way, the Dairycoates flyover being ready to open in 1962 followed by Boulevard in 1965. Then gradually diversions and the Beeching rail closures almost completely swept away a problem that had plagued Hull for decades.

The old Dolcis shoe shop being removed to make way for a more modern structure in keeping with, and part of, the Triangle Trust block development seen on the right. Photograph by courtesy of Sam Allon Collection.

1956

The year that:-

The Queen laid the foundation stone for a new Coventry Cathedral.

Third Class travel on British Railways was abolished to conform to continental practice.

Britain's first nuclear power station went into operation at Calder Hall.

Britain and America were linked by sub-marine transatlantic telephone cable.

Britain and France ordered an invasion of Egypt after President Nasser seized the Suez Canal.

Premium bonds first went on sale.

Hits like Bill Haley's 'Rock around the Clock' and Elvis Presley's 'Hound Dog' brought the American rock n' roll craze to Europe.

JANUARY.

8th   Telephone lines were brought down all over Hull when a severe storm swept the area. Any further expansion of the system was halted for a fortnight while engineers attended to the repairs.

9th   The death occurred of Alderman Alfred Kyno Jacobs, considered by many to be one of the most controversial figures in the history of Hull City Council. A prominent member of the Municipal Association Group and Lord Mayor in 1952-3, he left funds in his will to build the Esther Jacobs Homes in memory of his mother.

Workmen were busy filling in the **Peter Pan Lake in East Park**. The once popular children's pool had fallen into disrepair and there were complaints that it had become a breeding ground for mosquitoes.

A worrying drop in coal tonnage passing through Hull was reported. Coal was one of the port's key export commodities but the amount shipped during 1955 was over a million tons down on the year

before, reflecting the changing export markets. The steep decline continued for the rest of the decade.

To improve city centre road safety, new traffic islands were being experimented with at the top of Whitefriargate and in Queen Victoria Square. Footpaths were being widened and barriers erected to encourage pedestrians to use the crossings. Meanwhile traders on Holderness Road raised a petition in response to new parking restrictions, introduced after the Chief Constable became concerned about the long delays to peak hour traffic. They claimed the loss of passing trade was hitting business by as much as 25%. Instead of a complete ban they called for single-side parking for up to 20 minutes on alternate days.

FEBRUARY.

8th   Only hours after building work costing £30,000 was finished the Bishop of Whitby, the very Rev. Philip Wheeldon, consecrated **St. Alban's Church** in Hall Road, an imposing yet dignified red-brick landmark designed by Messrs. Milner & Craze. Work had started on the much needed facility in 1938 but the war intervened to prevent its completion. The structure then deteriorated so badly that it had to be started almost afresh. Its interior was described as a fine example of modern church architecture.

10th   A new **Woolworths Super Store in King Edward Street**, forming the central feature of a parade of shops being developed by Ravenseft Properties Ltd., opened to the public after a preview for the Lord Mayor and Sheriff. The store had a street frontage of 118 ft., counter displays totalling 1,500 ft. in length and one of the largest food sections in the North of England. The main contractors were Sir Robert McAlpine (Newcastle-upon-Tyne) Ltd.

Demolition workers were in action high above one of Hull's busiest streets - Carr Lane - dismantling the **Grosvenor Hotel**, a massive edifice designed by Sir Wm. Alfred Gelder in 1891.

MARCH.

15th   The latest branch of the **Hull Savings Bank** and its fifteenth within the city boundary, opened near the shopping centre in Greenwich Avenue to serve the Bilton Grange and Longhill districts. It was the work of local architects Messrs. Wheatley & Houldsworth.

26th   W.H. Smith's started a lending library on the first floor of their King Edward Street branch. New books could be borrowed

Jervis High School, Bilton Grange. To the general public, much 1950s architecture seemed to consist of plain concrete and glass 'boxes'. Here, an attempt was made to introduce a touch of individuality by using patterned brickwork.

Stage one of Bladons store in Prospect Street. Hull's new city centre provoked mixed feelings. Some praised its clean, sweeping lines while others said the buildings were dull and lacked imagination. Given the shortage of money and materials, it probably represented the best that could be achieved. Photograph by courtesy of Innes Studios, Hessle.

Fish aplenty on the quayside ready for the Easter Trade. Served by 150 modern deep sea trawlers, Hull was arguably the world's largest fishing port. By the late 1950s trawlers lost in minesweeping duties had been replaced with larger vessels equipped with every scientific aid for catching and navigating. There were daily landings of up to 1,000 tons of fish from the distant waters of Greenland, Bear Island, the White Sea and Iceland. With around 50,000 people directly or indirectly connected with the fishing industry, one-sixth of the population depended on its fortunes. Photograph by courtesy of Innes Studios, Hessle.

for sixpence each and older ones for threepence or you could take out an annual subscription for 25/- or 12/6 respectively.

28th BBC and ITV cameras were recording landing and market scenes at Hull Fish Dock on its busiest day of the year, the traditional Holy Week 'Show Day'. Trawlers began landing their catches at 2 a.m., vessels double-banking in the dock to enable them to come speedily alongside as soon as each one was discharged. Fifteen trawlers managed to catch the market: seven from Icelandic grounds, four from Bear Island, two from the Norwegian coast and two from the Faroes as well as three Danish seiners, making a total offering of 293,650 stones of fish. The usual 11 fish trains were augmented with extras right up to 9 p.m. to get the haul away to the inland markets. After some years 'in the doldrums' prosperity was returning again to Hull Fish Market. Landings for the first four days of Holy Week reached 917,000 stones - a postwar record - just failing to meet 1937's figure of over a million.

Slowly but surely Hull's well-known city centre stores were being rehabilitated after coping for over a decade in temporary prefabricated huts. The latest to complete the initial stage of rebuilding was **Bladons Ltd**. on the corner of Prospect Street and Spencer Street. The three-storey building had partially reopened at Christmas with displays of furniture, carpets, linoleum, soft furnishings and household linens and was soon to have a café on the top floor. The adjacent huts were now being torn down to enable the next stage to be finished by the year end. At the Spencer Street side work was in progress on a new public house to be known as the **Spencer Arms**.

Demolition of the 180 ft. high tower and spire of the old **St. Stephen's Church** went ahead after an attempt to preserve it failed. The church authorities had offered it to Hull Corporation as a monument but the Town Planning Committee could not justify spending £15,000 to restore the fractured, leaning structure. With no church for support it would have needed buttressing and it was considered to be of no special architectural merit, just a familiar landmark.

A survey by Careers Guidance staff showed that practical work was the most popular choice of the 800 girls and boys leaving Hull schools at Easter. The boys preferred the skilled trades such as electrician, welder or fitter while the girls opted first for factory work and then dressmaking, laundry work, printing or food and drink manufacture. Shop and office work was last on their lists. One-third of Eastfield School's boy leavers chose the fishing industry, another third favoured skilled trades while the rest became office boys, van boys or lorrydriver's mates. With more jobs available than school leavers to fill them there was no unemployment problem among young people.

APRIL.

1st The 32-acre **Princess Elizabeth Playing Fields** on Beverley High Road opened to the public for the first time on Easter Sunday. Sadly within two months they were badly vandalised. Initials were carved on woodwork, concrete posts around the cricket pitch were pushed over and young trees, shrubs and roses snapped off.

4th A 100 yard-long section of No 1 Quay at Hull Fish Market caved in during the night and had to be roped off. The subsidence was believed to be a legacy of the war when a landmine fell nearby and damaged quayside piling.

6th H.R.H. The Duke of Edinburgh spent the morning in the city to re-open the modernised and extended **Hull Trinity House Navigation School**. The Duke was installed as an Honorary Brother of Trinity House in the rush-strewn council room according to an ancient tradition created by past master mariners.

16th Over 200 members of the Hull Young People's Christian and Literary Institute (the Y.P.I.) voted in favour of a plan to hand it over to the Corporation. The 95 year old body, with meeting rooms in George Street and a sports club in Ferens Avenue, had a mounting debt problem with losses totalling £6,666 over four years.

28th The Sheriff of Hull laid the foundation stone of the new **Clowes Memorial Methodist Church**, Greenwood Avenue. The church, being built to replace a temporary one, was named after William Clowes, the Primitive Methodist pioneer from the Potteries who had made Hull his headquarters in 1819. Population drift had caused the first Clowes Chapel in Jarratt Street to close in 1931 and it was now a warehouse.

Hull Central Library was not to be left behind by the march of technology. There were plans to buy a machine to photograph the details of a book and reader's ticket on to microfilm, which would not only reduce queues but also save stationery and the salary of an assistant.

With the second television channel likely to reach Hull in the autumn, Housing Committee members were worried about the impact of ITV aerials on the townscape. As well as the unsightly

H.R.H. The Duke of Edinburgh inspecting cadets at Hull Trinity House during a visit in April 1956 to mark his installation as an Honorary Brother of the ancient institution. In the background is the School Headmaster Mr. E. R. Eddon. Photograph by courtesy of the Wardens and Brethren of the Corporation of the Hull Trinity House.

Throwing coins into the fountain at Fletchers Corner quickly became a favourite pastime of children 'going into town' with their parents. In the first two years, more than £2,000 was collected and used to fund a senior citizens' outing. Photograph by courtesy of Hull City Council Department of Planning and Design.

appearance of the 'colossal set up' of five uprights alongside the BBC H or X formation it was feared they would impose a strain on the chimney stacks of Corporation houses. Some members thought master aerials, one to a block, would be the best solution.

MAY.

1st An ornamental fountain at the corner of Jameson Street and King Edward Street came into operation, creating a pleasant oasis amid the bustling city streets. During construction there was much speculation and public comment, some likening it to a giant bird bath and criticising the 'waste of ratepayer's money'. In fact it was paid for in full by Ravenseft, the developers of what was to become **'Fletchers Corner'**. Perhaps inspired by a recent film about Rome's famous Trevi fountain, people quickly developed the habit of throwing coins into the water which were collected frequently and used to fund pensioners' treats. Not long afterwards nine boys were accused of stealing from the fountain and an unusual case turned on the question of who the coins belonged to. It was decided they were the property of the Corporation.

16th The Lord Mayor opened **Wilton House**, Holderness Road, the latest home for 37 elderly people and the fifth to open during his year of office.

27th Thos. Hamling & Co.'s newest trawler the *St. Celestin* (H233), built at Beverley in 1952, sank near Bear Island (south of Spitzbergen) shortly after colliding with the *Arctic Viking*, another Hull vessel. All the crewmen were rescued.

Hull F.C. were riding on the crest of a wave after finishing the season in fourth place in the Rugby League and beating Halifax 10-9 in the Championship play-off final at Manchester City's ground. Earlier they had reached the final of the Yorkshire Cup, drawing 10-10 against Halifax at Headingley but losing the Odsal replay 0-7. Meanwhile Hull City were going through a barren period, facing a spell in Division Three North after ending up 22nd in the table. Not even the efforts of gifted striker Bill Bradbury, brought to City by their new manager Bob Brocklebank, were enough to stave off relegation.

As work finally got under way on a project to bring water to the city from a new source on the River Hull (*see page 70*), the original Springhead pumping station was being converted from steam to diesel and electric power. Two steeplejacks from Sheffield were engaged on the tough job of demolishing the 120 ft. high chimney.

With brickwork 30" wide at the top and 6 ft. thick at the base, it was built to last for ever. The old triple-expansion steam engine was phased out and it was also decided to preserve as a museum piece the massive Cornish beam engine named after Alderman Woodhouse in 1876.

Reckitts bought out the old-established paint and varnish makers Sissons Bros. & Co. Ltd. of Bankside for £1 million in cash.

It was decided to offer Hull children vaccination against polio, a disease which had remained active in the city since a big outbreak in 1947. Surprisingly parents were slow to take advantage and after two months only 703 children were registered out of a possible 30,000.

JUNE.

1st A luncheon was held at the Guildhall to celebrate the centenary of local firm T.J. Smith & Nephew Ltd. From a tiny chemists shop opened by Thos. James Smith at 61 Whitefriargate they had grown steadily into an international group employing over 4,000 people and become world-famous for Elastoplast first-aid dressings, Nivea cream and numerous other medical and surgical products.

17th The **Barham Hotel** in Marfleet Lane was the latest public house to serve the people of East Hull. Designed by Mr. W. Edwin Thompson of Moors & Robsons Brewery and built by Stan Spruit, it had a lounge, smokeroom, bar, off licence, living quarters and a car park. The hand painted inn sign depicted a three-masted frigate - the *Barham* - in line with the street-naming theme of Bilton Grange.

After using a piano for 14 years Queens Road Methodist Church broke new ground by being the first Hull church with an electronic organ.

Construction of a 440 yard seven-lane running track was well under way at **Costello Playing Fields**. Costing £4,000 it promised to be one of the finest in the North of England and was to be administered jointly by Hull Corporation and representatives of the national athletics bodies. Runners would pay 6d. a day or 5/- a season.

JULY.

25th Church redevelopment in Hull was proceeding apace, the latest to open being **St. Wilfrid's** in the Boulevard. The old St.

Workmen removing the 'junk mountain' on Beverley Road, a frequent topic of conversation over the years. The children of the district watch with typical inquisitiveness. Photograph by courtesy of Hull City Council Department of Planning and Design.

The scene at St. Andrew's Dock after the fish quay caved in on 4th April 1956. A wartime landmine was believed to have caused a weakness to develop in the dock wall. Photograph by courtesy of Innes Studios, Hessle.

During 1956 the enormous Victorian Grosvenor Hotel in Carr Lane was pulled down in order to create another much-needed temporary car park. Telephone House was eventually built on the site. Photograph by courtesy of Hull City Record Office.

The Lord Mayor, Alderman Harry Kneeshaw (right), making a presentation to Mr. Herbert Morrison CH MP on his appointment as High Steward of Kingston upon Hull. The former Foreign Secretary in the Labour Government became the 23rd holder of the ancient office. Photograph by courtesy of Innes Studios, Hessle.

Wilfrid's had been the only Roman Catholic church in the Middlesbrough Diocese to be completely razed to the ground during the war. With the benefit of a grant from Pope Pius XII the restored building incorporated several new features including high-quality seating, an organ similar to one in the Vatican and a 'silent room' at the back where mothers with young children could hear Mass without disturbing other members of the congregation. Meanwhile the Reverend Wm. Watts of Queens Hall Methodist Mission declared it was time to close down 'useless and irrelevant down-town churches left high and dry by shift of population' and announced that a Commission would shortly be visiting Hull to present a plan for the redeployment of Methodist resources in the city. Ironically Hitler had assisted in the task: The Methodists lost 12 chapels in the war including one large mission hall.

As part of the British Railways Modernisation Plan **Botanic Locomotive Sheds** were being adapted for a new role, servicing the diesel locomotives and multiple units soon to be introduced in the Hull area. Botanic was to be a prototype for the larger depots at Dairycoates, York and Neville Hill (Leeds). During timing tests on the Hornsea and Withernsea lines two diesel units were found to be much faster than the existing steam-hauled trains. They were first 'unveiled' to the public at Withernsea Gala.

The City Council agreed to build a new straight road linking Lowgate with George Street to replace College Circle and its four radial roads. The idea was to release space for the new College of Technology block and provide a direct route for traffic diverted while Drypool Bridge was being rebuilt. It was the first new road scheme in Hull for 17 years.

AUGUST.

10th Mr. Frank Cousins (general secretary of the Transport & General Workers Union) came to Hull to open a new assembly hall at Bevin House, George Street. Named **Farmery Hall** after Alderman George Farmery, a pillar of the local Labour Movement until his death in a motor accident in 1942, the 500 seat hall became a popular venue for union meetings, rallies, lectures, concerts and dances.

Two familiar landmarks were disappearing from the city centre scene: An ornamental archway in Carr Lane through which hundreds of lorries had driven to **Jarman & Flint's** (one of the area's biggest importers and produce handlers) until bombing forced them to move to Cottingham; and a public clock on buildings being pulled down at the King Edward Street/Jameson Street corner, a well-used time check for workers hurrying to their offices in a morning.

Densely-populated Bean Street (said to have more residents than the whole of Withernsea) gained the distinction of being Hull's first 'play street'. All through traffic was prohibited between the hours of sunrise and sunset.

The end came at last for a junk mountain which for long enough had disfigured the appearance of Beverley Road. Mr. Edward Grocock, a scrap dealer who seemed to be more expert at buying than selling, was served with a notice under the Town & Country Planning Act after complaints from neighbouring businesses had been discussed by the authorities for years. Nine men and 53 lorry loads were needed to shift the rusty mountain of bedsteads, bicycles, chairs, mirrors and other lumber that covered the forecourt. Despite the jumble Mr. Grocock invariably managed to find an article his customers wanted.

SEPTEMBER.

9th   One of the most serious peacetime fires at the port of Hull occurred aboard the Swedish timber ship ss. *Lona* berthed at No. 12 Quay in King George Dock. The flames quickly spread through the engine-room and among the cargo of Canadian pitprops. After a tricky operation lasting 12 hours, they were finally extinguished after lowering the water level in the dock and sinking the vessel on to the bottom.

14th   The Archbishop of York dedicated the new **St. Cuthbert's Church** in Marlborough Avenue. The 200 seat church cost £15,000 and replaced an iron structure dating from 1906. It was designed by church choir member Mr. Douglas Potter in fulfilment of a lifetime's ambition.

14th   **Fletchers**, the bakers, pork butchers and provisions dealers, opened a large store at the corner of Jameson Street and King Edward Street.

24th   Daring smash and grab raiders paid a dawn visit to Carmichaels store and snatched over 70 rings and 12 cameo brooches worth £2,500 in Hull's biggest jewel robbery for many years. They were scared off by a milkman at 4.40 a.m. and left over £1,000 worth of antique jewellery on the pavement. Police set up road blocks on all exit routes.

26th A free lecture entitled 'Childbirth Without Fear' by Dr. Grantley Dick Read, a nationally-known advocate of natural childbirth, attracted a capacity audience of 1,800 to Queens Hall. Perhaps reflecting the modern view of childbirth as a family affair many of the women were accompanied by their partners, although some of the men apparently fainted and had to be given first aid by the nurses present! The lecture was so popular that it was repeated in April 1957 to a full City Hall.

28th During the afternoon more than 50 yards of dock wall supporting the fish quay at St. Andrew's Dock suddenly collapsed, sending hundreds of tons of bricks and concrete crashing into the dock. Fortunately no one was near the danger area.

The latest manual operation to be automated was the back-breaking task of shovelling coal from railway wagons into sacks. Revell Bros. became the first merchants in Yorkshire to introduce mechanical grabs and bag-filling machines at their Abbey Street yard. A crew of three, loading a hopper and controlling the flow of coal down electrically vibrated chutes into sacks, could dispose of 20 tons an hour, previously an average day's work.

Hull was suffering from a plague of unruly Teddy Boys. Groups of crew-cutted, narrow-trousered youths, brawling and shouting insults at passers-by, were making parts of the city centre unpleasant places to venture into at night. The Rock 'n' Roll craze, sparked off by a film featuring the hit 'Rock Around the Clock', was causing similar problems all over Britain. Hull's Watch Committee voted by 8 to 3 to ban the film after the Chief Constable warned of possible trouble among the city's normally well-behaved adolescents.

OCTOBER.

11th The Lord Mayor announced that the Queen had approved the appointment of Mr. Herbert Morrison CH MP as High Steward of Kingston upon Hull. The office was first held by Sir Francis Walsingham in 1583 and had lain vacant since the death of Mr. T.R. Ferens in 1930.

13th Despite objections from Hull's shopkeepers the Council decided to allow Hull Fair to open for two Saturdays (starting on 13th and ending on 20th) instead of the usual six day period from the historic Hull Fair Day - October 11th. Since 1952 the fair had been granted an extra Saturday by adding a day at the beginning or end but this was the first complete break with tradition. The Corporation was looking to increase its rent revenue but the

Chamber of Trade claimed that the fair took thousands of pounds worth of business away from the city's shops. The debate, acrimonious at times, raged on annually well into the 1960s.

17th Princess Alexandra of Kent made her first visit to Hull to declare open the new **YWCA House** in Princes Avenue. She was conducted round by Mrs J.B. Upton, President of Hull YWCA. The purpose of the £32,000 hostel was to provide a low-cost home for up to 40 girls and women who had come to Hull to find work.

Hull's museum displays were being reorganised. The Mortimer Collection of prehistoric archaeology was removed from the City Hall to High Street where all collections (except Maritime) were being centralised. The vacated space was to become an exhibition suite - the **Victoria Galleries**.

Lord Mackintosh (Chairman of the National Savings Movement) praised Hull as one of the best savings centres in the U.K. Since 1940 Hull people had saved £135 millions and the city held pride of place for the highest savings per head of population. He was speaking at the Movement's 40th anniversary social at the Guildhall.

Carlines 'Cash and Carry' self-service grocery stores were springing up all over Hull.

Production had begun in the new engineering shops of **J.H. Fenner & Co. Ltd.** of Marfleet, built and equipped at a cost of £350,000 to manufacture mechanical power transmission gear, much of it for export. A number of key workers had transferred to Hull from their Heckmondwike factory but many more were recruited locally.

NOVEMBER.

3rd Britain's second television channel - ITV - was brought into 250,000 Yorkshire homes, including the Hull area, at 7 p.m. when the 200 Kw Emley Moor transmitter (the most powerful in the country) was switched on. The programmes were supplied by Granada TV during the week and ABC Television at weekends andcomprised a mixture of variety shows, panel games, 'give away' shows, newscasts and sports reports, laced with commercial advertising. Reception was said to be generally good throughout the East Riding though slightly dimmed in the city centre where the signal was masked by high buildings.

11th Alderman W. Fox, Deputy Lord Mayor, unveiled the **Oppy Wood Memorial** stone at the Cenotaph, a replica of those marking the site where the East Yorkshire Regiment met and attempted to turn back the Germans in one of the fiercest battles of World War I.

12th   Undaunted by the worrying omen cast nine days earlier by the arrival of ITV, Mr. Brinley Evans (chairman/managing director of Hull Cinemas) watched as the Lord Mayor opened the **Berkeley** in Greenwich Avenue, Hull's second post-war cinema. The amenity appeared to be welcomed by the Bilton Grange and Longhill residents who lived a long way from city centre attractions. A telegram of good wishes was received from Marilyn Monroe, star of the opening feature 'Bus Stop'. Designed by Messrs. Gelder & Kitchen and built in nine months by Spooners Ltd., the cinema could seat 1,200 and had full air conditioning, stereo sound and a wide screen. The exterior was kept plain to allow more money to be spent on internal comforts for patrons.

21st   Queues formed at petrol stations and 'sold out' notices appeared by mid-morning as a wave of panic buying hit Hull the day before ration books were issued at Post Offices in response to the Suez crisis. To save fuel Hull Corporation Transport made urgent plans to cut 4,500 weekly motorbus miles by restricting evening and weekend services and stepping up the use of trolleybuses. Within days the queues had gone, a price rise of 1/5d. a gallon having forced most motorists off the road, and the city's streets took on a semi-permanent Sunday morning appearance.

There was swift public reaction to the recent placing of four telephone kiosks and parking spaces for cars at Monument Bridge. It was claimed the 'monstrosities' spoilt the fine view of the City Hall from Whitefriargate and obstructed foot traffic.

Priory Baptist Church, Coronation Road, was officially opened by Mrs G. Williamson with a key presented to her by the architect Mr. H.J. Hollingsworth.

A. Brown & Sons opened one of the largest walk-round bookshops in the country at 24-8 George Street.
Hull fishing industry interests were dismayed when Britain finally accepted the extension of Iceland's territorial waters to four miles after a prolonged dispute. In January 1957 the trawler *Isolfur* became the first Icelandic vessel to land fish at Hull for 4½ years.

DECEMBER.

3rd   The first stage in the development of the colleges complex at the east end of Queens Gardens was reached when Lord Hives (Chairman of Rolls-Royce Ltd.) opened a £312,000 Workshop Block to house the various building and engineering departments of **Hull College of Technology**. The single-storey reinforced concrete structure with a saw-tooth roof, built by Wm. Moss & Sons Ltd., would within a few years be hidden behind an eight-storey main building, the end product being one of the finest college complexes in the North of England.

10th   **Gipsyville's new permanent Library** at the corner of Hessle High Road and North Road was officially opened by Alderman Sydney Smith, replacing a part-time facility at nearby Francis Askew School. It was stocked with 14,000 books and housed Hull's second children's library.

The White Horse, a Bass Worthington public house in Carr Lane, opened after a rebuilding project had given it a modern neo-Georgian appearance. There had been an inn on the site since 1791 and in bygone days it was one of Hull's foremost theatrical taverns.

With road traffic increasing at a far faster rate than ever expected the Town Planning Committee were getting restless over the Minister of Transport's refusal to sanction spending on a much-needed road linking Paragon Square with Osborne Street, together with a roundabout in front of the Cecil cinema. Chairman Alderman Body declared, 'We should put our foot down over these delays to our major road schemes.'

1950s CHURCH ARCHITECTURE :

Photographs by courtesy of :

1 & 2 Hull City Council Department
of Planning and Design
3 & 4 Innes Studios, Hessle.

1 : Derringham Bank
Methodist Church,
Willerby Road / Spring
Bank West.

2 : Clowes Memorial
Methodist Church,
Greenwood Avenue.

*3 : St. Thomas' Church,
Louis Drive / Hotham Road.*

*4 : The Danish Church
of St. Nicholai,
Osborne Street.*

HULL BUSES - THE END OF A GOLDEN AGE.

The immediate post-war years have been described as the 'golden age' of public transport. Private motoring was restricted by petrol rationing and a scarcity of cars (with 75% going for export new cars were taking three years to deliver on the home market in 1950). Buses were fully stretched catering not only for the masses of workpeople but also hordes of cinemagoers and football spectators, with interest in these pastimes at an all-time high. Hull's Corporation Transport undertaking (KHCT) had extended its network to serve all the new housing estates and in 1948 the number of passengers peaked at 102 millions. It was financially sound and year after year returned profits to the coffers of the City Council.

It was a very different story in the 1950s. The city's two main bus operators became locked into a downward spiral of higher operating costs and higher fares chasing an ever shrinking market.

In Hull their main competitor was not the car but the bicycle. The flat terrain encouraged pedal cycling while the growing popularity of mopeds and motorised cycles resulted from easy Hire Purchase terms and their fuel economy - 100 m.p.g. being common. A 1955 survey showed that 17,600 people entered the city centre by bus each morning peak compared with 12,700 by cycle and only 2,600 by car. Little wonder Hull was dubbed 'Cycle City' and Mr. G. Pulfrey (KHCT's general manager) was said to pray regularly for rain! Bus operation was also becoming more expensive as the population drifted outwards to the widely spread suburbs.

In 1954, with KHCT facing a deficit of £80,000, a package of economy measures was brought in. Reluctantly the Transport Committee had already accepted advertisements on the sides of their smart blue and white buses to increase revenue. Now a programme of mileage cuts and a 2d. minimum fare were proposed. The cuts, especially the withdrawal of the No. 21 bus route along Cottingham Road, caused an immediate wail of public protest with petitions and letters of objection coming from bodies as diverse as business firms, Hull Trades Council and the local Communist Party. Nevertheless they achieved their objective and in 1955 a surplus of £44,000 was made despite a four million drop in passengers. Such results were unlikely to be repeated however and a more radical solution was called for.

Mr. Pulfrey had been interested for some time in the possibility of one-man operated double-decker trolleybuses and Hull's distinctive 'Coronation' class Sunbeams were custom-built to his specification

with this idea in mind. In July 1956 trials began with a 'magic eye' sited on the entry and exit staircases to inform the driver, by means of an indicator box in the cab, how many seats were available on the top deck. This device together with an American-style farebox would have made one-man operation feasible but problems in obtaining Ministry of Transport permission and disquiet from the busmen's union about one man doing the work of two eventually proved insurmountable.

With single-decker motorbuses however one-man operation was a simpler proposition. Two AEC Regal 35-seaters were modified at the Liverpool Street works by altering the driver's side window to take a payments tray and fitting driver-controlled doors. Three lightly used services (No. 52 - Saltend to Preston; No. 28 - Queens Road to Chapman Street and No. 19 - Coach Station to Sutton Road) were chosen to launch the experiment on 18th January, 1954.

The scheme appeared to go well and in 1957 the Transport Committee authorised its extension using ten specially purchased AEC Reliance saloons. A 15% pay bonus was offered to tempt drivers to volunteer for solo duties. However the men, worried about the prospect of mass job losses, voted 476-64 against the plans and a lengthy, at times acrimonious, dispute ensued which was eventually referred to arbitration. KHCT were finally given the green light early in 1958 and the Reliances, which had been marking time as peak-hour extras, were used in their intended role from 18th May on the lightly trafficked routes to Bricknell Avenue (No. 14), Hedon, Paull and Wawne.

East Yorkshire Motor Services, the principal operator serving the rural areas from Hull, was also going through difficult times. By 1958 profits had fallen to £10,850 on a revenue exceeding £1 million, squeezed on the one hand by falling passengers and on the other by a crippling 200% fuel tax. Fare rises were applied for every year between 1953 and 1959 and no fewer than three times in 1957, much to the disgust of the travelling public in the East Riding.

Falling revenue and rising costs led to the introduction of 'pay as you enter' single-deck buses, with the driver collecting the fares. Photograph by courtesy of Kingston upon Hull City Transport Ltd.

Hull's nickname 'Cycle City' was never more apt than in the 1950s. Thousands regularly travelled to work by bicycle and cycle clubs were an important leisure interest. There were dozens of cycle dealers, some like Cliff Pratt actually assembling their own bikes. Photograph by courtesy of Innes Studios, Hessle.

The staff of Thompson of Hull Ltd. showing off the latest Vauxhall Victor motor cars outside their Anlaby Road premises in 1958. Photograph by courtesy of Innes Studios, Hessle.

1957

The year that:-

Eden resigned as Prime Minister and was succeeded by Harold Macmillan.

The European Common Market treaty was signed by France, Germany, Italy and the Benelux countries.

Britain's first H-Bomb was exploded near Christmas Island.

Russia launched a dog into space in Sputnic II.

The largest radio telescope in the world went into operation at Jodrell Bank.

Ninety people died in a rail accident in fog at Lewisham.

The Queen's Christmas broadcast was televised for the first time.

JANUARY.

7th   Steam power gave way to diesel multiple unit trains on local passenger services between Hull and Beverley, Hornsea, Withernsea, Brough and Goole. Driver Ernest Train took out the first two-car unit on the 52 minute run to Withernsea. Powered by two 150 h.p. underfloor motors each train could carry 12 first-class and 103 second-class passengers. For the drivers it meant cleaner working conditions and, as the units could be driven from either end, train movements were simplified at Paragon Station where the dead-end had required frequent shunting of engines.

Workmen were pulling down the old **Phillips Chambers** in Anne Street to create extra car parking space. Eventually the site was destined to house the civic telephone headquarters.

At the turn of a 'phone dial, pop music fans could listen to a hit record, selected weekly by a local store, when the Corporation Telephone Department introduced 'Teledisc', the latest in a series of recorded information services to be brought in following the successful Father Christmas link in 1952. Others available were 'Phonodiary' (a guide to local entertainments); the Speaking Clock; Telechef (a daily recipe) and a Test Match Score Service.

W.H. Smith & Sons opened one of the North's biggest and most modern newspaper, book and stationery distribution centres at **Hambledon House** in Canning Street. The 30,000 sq.ft. plain red-brick building built by F.R. Shepherd & Son Ltd. replaced their blitzed premises in Jameson Street.

FEBRUARY.

1st   With the driving of the first of 1,600 piles work began in earnest on reconstructing the **Riverside Quay** and the south side of Albert Dock. The main contract had been won by A. Monk & Co. Ltd. who used a type of pile - a 3" thick pre-stressed hollow bar - never previously employed in this country. Progress was delayed however when the remains of an earlier quay were discovered 50ft. below ground. At the same time the old Riverside Quay clock tower, a familiar dockside landmark and lone survivor of the blitz, succumbed to the demolition hammers.

7th   The City Architect revealed to the Council plans for two 12-storey blocks of flats on Anlaby Road. They would be the tallest residential buildings in Hull and set the pattern for central housing redevelopment over the next 25 years.   Together with four and seven-storey blocks they would fill an empty strip between Walker Street and Convent Lane, housing 1,000 people in less than 8 acres of land. To create a smoke-free environment the flats would be heated by radiators from a central boilerhouse and have dustbin chutes for refuse disposal. A model of the project, which formed part of a comprehensive plan for **'Residential Area 17'** (the area bounded by Hessle Road, Anlaby Road and Bean Street), was put on show at Ferens Art Gallery.

There was grave concern about the state of one of Hull's ancient churches - **St. Mary's, Lowgate**. It was said to be in danger of falling into ruins, the troubles including crumbling stone work, worn-out piers, Death Watch Beetle in the roof, rotting pew platforms and damp floors. The erosion of the limestone was blamed on the city's industrial atmosphere. An appeal was launched to raise £20,000 to save and restore the building.

After transferring the swans and ducks to other parks, **West Park Lake** was being filled in and the area transformed into a children's playground and paddling pool.

A new diesel multiple-unit train preparing to leave Paragon Station early in 1957. The passing of the steam engines they replaced was not without regret but most travellers appreciated the improved comfort, cleanliness and speed. Photograph by courtesy of Innes Studios, Hessle.

Perhaps one of the most altered scenes in modern Hull : The Jameson Street/ Bond Street corner. Not only have the 'Tally Ho' public house and the old Co-op premises gone but so have the Andrew Marvell statue and the ubiquitous trolleybus wires. Photograph by courtesy of Hull City Council Department of Planning and Design.

MARCH.

1st   **Woolworths** opened their fifth Hull branch at **455-7 Anlaby Road**. It was the first non-food store in the city to trade completely on self-service lines.

3rd   A final 'time' was called at the **'Tally Ho' public house** in Bond Street before it was pulled down to make way for road improvements designed to take the kink out of Bond Street.

4th   The Bishop of Middlesbrough opened the new Roman Catholic church of **Our Lady of Lourdes and St. Peter Chanel** on Cottingham Road. Designed by Mr. J. Houghton in a 'modern conventional Romanesque' style with a white statue of Our Lady above the front door, it cost £35,000.

6th   News of the death of the Town Clerk, Mr. Ernest H. Bullock, the day after his 46th birthday brought a touch of sadness to Hull. He had suffered ill health for some time and had to give up his duties for a while. An ex-Riley High School pupil, he started with the Corporation as an office boy and was appointed Town Clerk at the early age of 34. In 1944 he wrote a nationally-known book 'Planning Tomorrow's Britain'. His successor was Mr. J. Haydon W. Glen, the Town Clerk of Stockport.

11th   Another visible symbol of the new life being breathed into the city centre was the opening of **Leeds Permanent Building Society's** office block on the corner of Paragon Street and South Street. Designed by Elsworth Sykes & Partners and built by Messrs. Houlton & Grant, its curved corner featured a colourful abstract mosaic created by the Derbyshire sculptor Mr. Reginald Pope. Paragon Street was rapidly becoming colonised by building societies; in April the **Woolwich** was the latest to take up residence there from smaller premises at 29 Savile Street.

16th   Elsie Battle's well-known dress shop at 19 Jameson Street closed down prior to the sale of the property. Among the final bargains were wedding gowns for £5!

23rd   Sir Patrick Abercrombie, the eminent town planner who had been commissioned jointly with the late Sir Edwin Lutyens in 1942 to prepare plans for the post-war development of Hull, died aged 77.

31st   The Rt. Rev. Henry Townend Vodden, Bishop of Hull and Archdeacon of the East Riding since 1934, stepped down because of ill health. His successor was the Ven. George F. Townley. The Church of England was going through a process of change locally, the latest move being to unite the old-established Hessle Road parishes of St. James, St. Luke and St. Thomas to form an extended parish of Holy Trinity. **St. James' Church** closed at Easter, population drift having left it high and dry in an area now devoted to warehouses; the other two churches had never been fully restored after the war. In North Hull a novel experiment was launched to encourage young people to attend worship. On entry to church Fr. Gould (the new vicar of St. Mary's, Sculcoates) issued them with a ticket for a 90-minute Rock 'n' Roll session in the Parish Hall after Evensong.

The site was being prepared and drains laid for the new **Wilberforce Drive** link road.

APRIL.

11th   There was a bizarre sight at the back of Elm Street when three oil tankers were left rearing up wildly into the air after a coal train ran into them on the overhead railway line.

30th   During the afternoon **Hull City Police** relocated from five different offices in the city centre into their new **Queens Gardens headquarters**. Central Division locked up at Parliament Street for the first time since 1904; CID abandoned Grimston Drive and various other sections left Town Hall Chambers, the Guildhall and Municipal Buildings. Among the items to be moved were 100,000 finger prints, 15,000 photos of people and scenes of crimes, hundreds of uniforms and a massive stock of stationery. The new four-storey building was designed by Messrs. Priestman & Lazenby to conform to the overall plan for the Queens Gardens civic centre and built by F. Shepherd & Son Ltd. It was officially opened at 3.15 p.m. on Friday, 17th May by the Rt. Hon. H.S. Morrison MP, High Steward of Kingston upon Hull.

MAY.

18th   The whole of Hull was in a joyful mood: Crowds lined the pavements and many streets and prominent buildings were gaily decorated with Union Jacks and bunting for the visit of Her Majesty The Queen and H.R.H. The Duke of Edinburgh en route to Denmark for a state tour. During a hectic 6½ hour stay in the city the royal couple watched a trawler being discharged at the Fish Dock; visited the University; toured the Sailors Children's Homes and the Royal Infirmary; enjoyed a civic luncheon; saw the improvements taking place at King George Dock; rode in a land rover past a mass rally of 12,000 uniformed children from youth organisations throughout Hull and its neighbouring counties; and called to see the old people at Wilton House. Finally they embarked on the Royal Barge at Victoria Pier for a short sail into the Humber where the Royal Yacht 'Britannia' lay midstream off Alexandra Dock waiting to take them aboard. The Queen and Duke's farewell was marked by a 21 gun salute from a warship moored at the quayside. The complex 19 mile route and timetable resulted in much disruption to traffic flows in and around Hull and many bus and trolleybus services had to be diverted or cancelled, but the day left an impression that was long to remain in the memory of anyone who was present. Shortly afterwards a painting by the artist Terence Cuneo portraying The Queen's departure from the Pier was presented to the city for hanging in the Guildhall as a lasting memento.

21st   **Anchor House** on Anlaby Road, a recreational centre run by the Roman Catholic Apostleship of the Sea for seamen of all creeds and nationalities, was re-opened by Sir Richard Snedden (director of the Shipping Federation Ltd.) after receiving a new look. The centre, converted from what was once St. Mary's School gymnasium, had been extended at a cost of £27,000 to create a venue for dances and social functions of all kinds.

28th   Hull's Medical Officer of Health Dr. Alexander Hutchison and Health Committee Chairman Councillor W. Hobden called for smoking to be banned in all cinemas, theatres, restaurants and buses after research work had proved it to be linked with lung cancer. Smoking was already prohibited on the lower deck of Corporation buses.

31st   Mrs Basil Reckitt (the company chairman's lady) cut a tape to open a £60,000 pavilion at the Chamberlain Road sports ground of **Reckitt & Sons Ltd.**, a belated gift to the Hull employees to mark the firm's 1940 centenary. A crab-shaped building with a large central dining hall and four 'legs' branching off, it featured a games room, bar, 'teenagers alcove' and a giant 1,750 gallon bath capable of taking a full Rugby team. A feast of sporting action combined with warm, sunny weather to produce a happy occasion for the 2,000 employees and pensioners who attended with their families.

JUNE.

5th   Alderman H. Fairbotham opened **23-4 High Street**, a pair of Georgian Houses dating from around 1760 which the Corporation had saved from demolition and converted into Museum offices and showrooms. The **Transport Museum** nearby also opened for the first time since the war, following the restoration of all the exhibits.

13th   Mr. T.R. Ferens, a founder member of Hull Conservative Federation and grandson of one of Hull's greatest benefactors, became the first local man to be knighted for 28 years.

16th   Paragon Station was packed with people for several hours as the fine weather caused the biggest exodus to the seaside for 30 years. Nearly 11,000 boarded trains there during the morning for the five east coast resorts and half as many again went from the smaller urban stations. To cater for the demand British Railways had to lay on ten special trains in addition to the normal summer Sunday extras.

29th   More than 400 people squeezed into a building designed for 300 for the dedication of the new **Bricknell Avenue Methodist Church** by the Rev.J.R.Ridley (Hull Methodist District Chairman) after its opening by Miss Peggy Newlove, founder of the Sunday school. It was brick built on square, clean-cut lines with huge glass swing doors at the front. Behind the pulpit was a massive white cross set against a blue background. The society was formed in 1940 at the Newloves' West Bulls Farm and met for years in a former hen hut acquired for £350. By comparison the present development (including the 1953 church hall) cost £43,000. Now they had 300 regular worshippers and a Sunday school with 50 teachers and 500 scholars.

There was some embarrassment in local cultural circles when an exhibition of paintings by contemporary Danish artists opened at Ferens Art Gallery during an Anglo-Danish Festival. One of the civic party touring the exhibits objected to a painting depicting male and female nude figures and demanded its removal. Hull, it seemed, was not quite ready for art of this kind and after considerable discussion his wishes were respected but not before the incident had got into the papers. The next morning there was a long queue outside the gallery hoping to catch sight of the offending picture.

Workmen were putting the finishing touches to a new walled garden in **Pearson Park**.

Mr. Peter Goodman, conductor of Hull Bach Choir and music master at Kingston High School, was named as the new City Organist in succession to the late Mr. Norman Strafford.

...ne of the high spots of the decade for many citizens was the visit of Her Majesty The Queen and H.R.H. The Duke of Edinburgh on 18th May, 1957. Eleven ...ar old 'pirate chief' Anton Nielsen greeted the Royal couple with gifts on arrival at the Sailors' Childrens Society Homes at Newland during a hectic tour ...f the city. Photograph by courtesy of Innes Studios, Hessle.

Thornton-Varley's store in Prospect Street, decorated for The Queen's visit in May 1957. Photograph by Harry Cartlidge.

Traffic regulations posted up by the Chief Constable to assist him in his task of ensuring for the Royal visitors "a safe and orderly passage through the city". Photograph by Harry Cartlidge.

The War Damaged Sites Committee's purchase of a giant steam-roller for the Linnaeus Street adventure playground, in furtherance of their policy of providing exciting things for the youngsters to play with, was not quite the success hoped for. Protests soon came in from angry mothers tired of washing their offspring's clothes after contact with grease and dirt on the machine's cables and cogs!

JULY.

22nd Sam Allon Ltd. began to pull down the disused Tivoli Theatre. The job, which lasted until mid-August, was helped along by numerous souvenir hunters who took away bits of wood and stone and even doors from the much-loved building. The site had been purchased by local industrialist and Hull City chairman Mr. Harold Needler and piling was shortly to begin for a five-storey block of shops and offices.

26th The new **Humberside Pumping Station** was formally opened (*see page 115*).

29th East Yorkshire bus crews returned to work after a nine day strike, the first since the company was formed in 1926. The dispute concerned a reduction in pay differentials.

Pashby House, a new kind of club providing day care and rehabilitation for mentally disabled people who were unable to take up employment and for patients discharged from hospital but not quite ready for the demands of modern life, opened in the former James Reckitt Hostel in East Hull. It was named in tribute to Alderman W. Pashby OBE for his devoted services to mental health.

The restoration to former glory of a magnificent stained glass window in the banqueting hall of the Guildhall was completed 16 years after its tragic wartime destruction. The window depicted various coats of arms connected with the city of Hull but there was one variation on the original - the arms of the University had been added.

AUGUST.

1st A public inquiry opened at the Guildhall into plans by Hull Corporation to build on land west of Anlaby Park Road South to take families displaced by the slum clearance programme. The site, mainly occupied by four brickworks, was now capable of being developed as a result of the main drainage scheme. An estate for 5,000 people was envisaged with nearly 1,500 homes plus shops, schools and a public house. However fierce objections were raised by Haltemprice UDC and the East Riding County Council who claimed that it would destroy the separate identity of Hessle.

17th There was a riot at the Hedon Road Borstal Institution early in the morning when angry boys swarmed on to the roof hurling bricks and slates at warders below. In an attempt to get them down jets of water were directed at the youths by the Fire Brigade but they held out for 2½ hours before order was restored.

29th The Lord Mayor opened a new purpose-built branch of the **Hull Savings Bank** west of the Preston Road/Marfleet Lane junction. Founded in 1817 the Savings Bank was thriving in this most savings-conscious of all British cities. It had nearly 350,000 depositors' accounts holding total balances of over £35 millions. Interest rates on offer were 2½% in the Ordinary Department and 3-4¼% for Special Investment Accounts.

SEPTEMBER.

10th With the opening of **Wyke Hall** off Bricknell Avenue and **Newton Hall** at Greatfield, plans for a new system of secondary education in Hull were starting to take shape. Under the 'campus system' a group of three secondary schools - grammar, technical and secondary modern - would be built on adjacent sites, working closely together and permitting pupils to transfer freely from one course to another if their initial choice proved unsuitable. The idea was to allay parents' fears about the 11-plus settling too early the secondary education of their children. At Greatfield the 660 place technical school now opened was to be followed in September 1959 by a secondary modern for 450 pupils and later by a grammar for 530, all on one 44 acre site. Similarly there were plans to develop a campus in the Bricknell Avenue area taking in the existing Hull Grammar School, a proposal which brought immediate objections from the Old Grammarians who feared their identity would be submerged. The start of the school year also saw the opening of the **Riley High** and **Alderman Cogan Modern Schools** and the establishment of a new **Boulevard High School**. The latter allowed the senior boys' sections of four smaller schools - Constable Street, Chiltern Street, Somerset Street and Sir Henry Cooper - to close. Altogther Hull was budgeting for a 33% increase in places to cater for children born in the 'bulge years' now entering the secondary phase of schooling.

10th Spooners (Hull) Ltd. started work on one of the largest building projects yet seen in modern Hull, phase two of the **College**

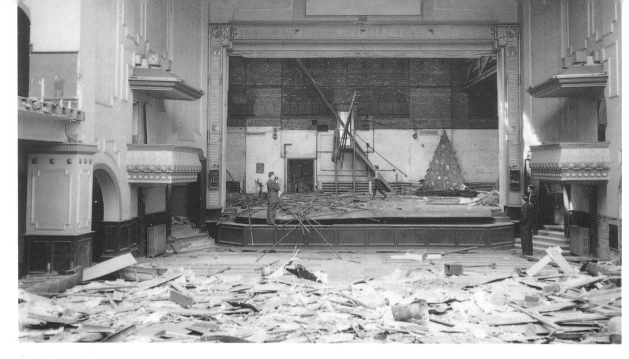

The demolition of the much-loved Tivoli Theatre in the summer of 1957 was a sad sight for many Hull people. Countless music hall stars had appeared there over the years including Arthur Lucan (Old Mother Riley) who died suddenly while waiting in the wings in 1954. Photograph by Harry Cartlidge.

Horne Brothers, a gents' outfitters and tailoring store, was a landmark on the corner of Jameson Street and Waltham Street. The property changed hands in 1957 in readiness for a large department store development. Photograph by courtesy of Hull City Council Department of Planning and Design.

of **Technology** facing Queens Gardens. Because of the poor ground conditions (the site being part of a filled in dock) the 290ft. long eight-storey block had to be built on a massive reinforced concrete slab supported by 530 concrete piles. It was expected to take three years to complete.

23rd   Three Hull High schools - Craven, Fifth Avenue and Riley - were among the first in the country to try an experimental BBC scheme to bring television to the classroom after being issued with 21" sets.

28th   Veteran Hull Methodist Mr. Thomas Platt and Mrs Luther Beal, wife of the builder, opened **Bilton Grange (Kingston Memorial) Methodist Church** in Nestor Grove. Built to the designs of Mr. B.W. Blanchard for £50,000, the splendid L-shaped suite of premises comprised a church for 350 worshippers, a hall with stage, three schoolrooms, vestries and a kitchen. The act of dedication was led by Rev. F. Pratt Green and the first preacher, Rev. F.G. Bromiley, had the distinction of also being the last to take the pulpit at the old Kingston Chapel in Witham. The church had been meeting in a nearby school for five years.

Some long-established businesses were about to be displaced to make way for development proposals. A big new department store was in prospect for Ferensway when C. & A. Modes Ltd. were granted a lease on the Corporation-owned site occupied by Mr. Sidney Zimmerman's furniture store and the Station tavern. Across the city centre Horne Brothers (a large tailoring store on the Jameson Street/King Edward Street corner) ceased trading after the property was acquired by the Co-op for incorporation into their new store.

There was an epidemic of Asian 'flu in the Hull area. At its peak on the 27th it caused 45% of all school children (24,300 pupils) to be away from their desks, compared with the normal absence rate of 8%. One in ten transport workers were affected and each night the buses had to be sprayed with disinfectant to damp down the germs. The outbreak disrupted local life in many ways: The big firms all suffered high rates of absenteeism, many football matches were cancelled, cinema attendances dropped and paper boys missed their rounds. One fatality was reported.

A familiar shipping name known in ports throughout the world for nearly three-quarters of a century - Cockerline of Hull - disappeared from the scene following the firm's liquidation. In the line's heyday 18 ships sporting red and black funnels and names ending in -ic (*Athenic*, *Majestic* etc.) had been engaged in worldwide tramping. The last one was sold 2-3 years earlier.

OCTOBER.

11th   Demolition of the bomb-ravaged **St. Mark-in-the-Groves church** began. Parishioners were continuing their worship in a converted house in Spyvee Street as many of the older people found it difficult to get to the nearest church - St. Saviour's at Stoneferry.

14th   The **King Edward VII public house**, which in pre-war days had been in the street of that name, was relocated to the corner of Anlaby Road and Anne Street. Designed by Gelder & Kitchen and built by Quibell & Son Ltd., it had an unorthodox two-floor layout.

18th   The first phase of a modernisation project was completed at **Regent Street Public Wash House**. The 20 year old washers and old pot sinks set in wooden draining boards had been stripped out and 16 modern gas-heated machines and aluminium sinks installed in their place. There was a constant supply of softened hot water and spin driers were now available for use. The Baths Committee considered the improvements justified in a neighbourhood where so many people still lived in tiny houses with only a poky back yard in which to do their weekly wash. However the changes were not all welcomed. There were moans and groans that fishermen's bags were not allowed; in the past women had made a living by washing them.

31st   Victoria Mansions in Passage Street, the Salvation Army Hostel for men, was renamed **William Booth House** after renovation.

Hull University was enjoying an upsurge in student numbers largely as a consequence of its 'promotion' from College status. Because only four academic buildings had been completed so far at Cottingham Road many lectures were having to be held in cold, draughty army-style huts dotted about the campus. There was also a housing problem. The Ferens and Cleminson Halls of residence at Cottingham could only cope with a fraction of those arriving from out of town but fortunately the Lodgings and Welfare Officer had a list of over 70 'landladies' in the city willing to offer students a bed, food and a family atmosphere for around £3 a week.

A public library was provided at **Longhill Primary School** three evenings a week to serve the 8,000 residents of Longhill Estate who were finding a big shortfall in social amenities compared with the areas they came from. Reading library books was certainly a popular pastime with Hull people in the 1950s. In the course of a year the city libraries lent four million books, a figure exceeded by only four other places - Manchester, Liverpool, Birmingham and Sheffield.

NOVEMBER.

Two of Hull's latest schools were officially inaugurated: On the 1st the **Riley Technical High School** in Parkfield Drive was opened by Mr. Eric Turner, chairman and managing director of Blackburn & General Aircraft Ltd. of Brough. The school had moved from the Boulevard where it had occupied the old Kingston High School buildings since 1941. Mr. Turner said it was the first of its type in Britain and messages of goodwill came from ex-students all over the world. Built by Robinson & Sawdon Ltd. to designs by the City Architect, it cost £250,000 and provided 660 places for boys studying courses to GCE level with a mainly scientific or engineering bias. The name commemorated Dr. J.T. Riley, the first principal of Hull Municipal Technical College with which the school was originally linked. A week later the **Alderman Cogan Secondary Modern** in Whitworth Street opened. The ceremony was performed by the Earl of Halifax with an act of dedication by the Archbishop of York. The 300 place school, designed by Messrs. Horth & Andrew and built by Markwell, Holmes & Hayter Ltd., had roots going back to 1755 when a school was endowed 'for the poor girls of the town'. Latterly it had been based in Park Street until in 1950 the premises were condemned. The foundation stone which had stood over the original school entrance was installed in the new assembly hall.

There were plans to instal an 'electronic brain' or computer in the City Treasury to allow the Corporation to keep up with technological progress in handling payroll, rates and other accounts.

DECEMBER.

4th   Mr. F.R. Metcalfe opened a new **Boulevard Police Boys Club** in Heron Street to provide boys with instruction in such leisure interests as boxing, P.T., woodwork, model-making and table tennis.

10th   The Junior Department of the **Holden Centre** in Leads Road, hailed as a milestone in the development of care for mentally handicapped children, was opened by Mr. R.H.M. Thompson, Parliamentary Secretary to the Minister of Health. Built on a three acre site to be laid out with lawns, gardens and playground equipment, it was named after Dr. John Fearne Holden (Hull's first Medical Officer of Health) and replaced a makeshift centre in Anlaby Road. Special buses collected up to 135 children daily from various pick-up points to take them to the new centre.

21st   The Bishop of Hull dedicated the **Church of St. Thomas** in Hotham Road South, the first to be built with money raised by the Humberside Churches Appeal. It had been cleverly designed to fit an awkwardly-shaped corner site by Mr. H. Roper Spencer. The temporary St. Chad's Mission Church in Wymersley Road could now be demolished.

Three new public houses were opened: **The Ganstead** (a Moors & Robsons house) at the junction of Ganstead Lane and Bilton Road, **The Georgian** (Bass Worthington of Burton) in George Street and **The Ravenser** (Joshua Tetley) at the corner of Southcoates Lane and Bedale Avenue. They replaced obsolete hostelries in the older parts of town in line with a plan to redistribute Hull's 250 or so licensed premises to areas where the bulk of the population now lived. The Porter Street area, for example, once had 31 public houses but would eventually have only four. Some of the old pub names set to disappear included The Queens Head (Walker Street), Fisherman's Arms (Adelaide Street), Leeds Arms (Porter Street), Abercrombie Hotel (Campbell Street) and Sheffield Arms (Hessle Road). The task of implementing the scheme fell to a Licensing Planning Committee comprising magistrates and Town Planning Committee members presided over by an independent chairman.

DANCE NIGHTS.

Hull was a mecca for Dance Band music in the 1950s. Popular dance venues, with some of the bands that entertained there, included:

The New York Hotel (*Harold Dawson and his Band*)
Jacksons Paragon Ballroom (*The Alan Bond Orchestra*)
Beverley Road Baths (*Harry Chatterton, Stan Thrussel, Leslie Rose*)
The Y.P.I. (*Tommy Fisher, Ken Brookes and Louis Gold*)
Blind Institute (*Norman Mail and his Band*)
City Hall (*various*)
Newington Hall (*The Newington Orchestra*)
East Hull Baths (*Maxwell Daniels and his Band*)

The bandsmen were always in great demand for big firms' functions as well as public dances held every Saturday night.

Women 'doing their chores' at the Public Wash-house in Regent Street off Hessle Road before modernisation in 1957. Places like this were important for fostering community spirit in a seagoing area where life was often a struggle and punctuated by occasional tragedy. Photograph by courtesy of Hull City Record Office.

The drainage scheme heralded the end of Hull's open drains which, often passing close to houses, threatened public health and safety. Filling-in of the Beverley & Skidby Drain, seen here alongside Fountain Road, began in 1958. Photograph by courtesy of Hull City Record Office.

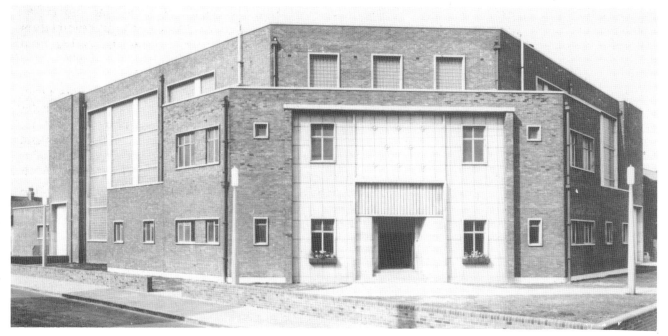

The Humberside Pumping Station took seven years to complete. With a deep underground sump, the structure is like an iceberg. Hull's 100 ft. high Wilberforce Monument would not be visible at the top if placed inside. Photograph by courtesy of Hull City Record Office.

DRAINING A CITY.

The opening of the Humberside Pumping Station by Mr. Henry Brooke, Minister of Housing and Local Government, at 11 a.m. on 26th July, 1957 marked a significant stage in one of the largest civil engineering projects ever seen in the area - Hull's deep drainage scheme.

For over twenty years the inadequacy of Hull's drainage to meet modern demands had been all too apparent. The existing drains were overloaded while some outylying areas were not even connected to the public sewer. The Victorian pumping stations at Harrow Street and Hedon Road were reaching the end of their economic life.

These deficiencies seriously hindered the Corporation's efforts to open up vast expanses of land for new housing development in order to rid the city of its thousands of obsolete, overcrowded and sub-standard homes. Industrial expansion was also being thwarted, in particular plans for a trading estate in the Sutton Road area.

Then there was the flooding problem which recurred with menacing regularity two or three times almost every winter. Hull's level, low-lying ground rendered it extremely susceptible to floods especially when heavy rain coincided with high tides, causing storm water to 'back up' through the drains and overflow into the streets, subways and cellars. The problem was literally brought home to many residents in the Old Town and Cleveland Street areas one weekend in November 1954 when 1,400 families suffered the distress of flood water penetrating their homes. It was also a particular nuisance at Chanterlands Avenue and Boothferry Road where the subways beneath the railway bridges would fill up with water forcing the temporary diversion of road traffic.

As a related issue, several miles of agricultural drains passed through the built-up areas on their way to the River Hull posing not only a threat to public health from stagnant water, mosquitoes and so on during the summer but also a danger to small children for whom, armed with tiddler nets and jam jars, they tended to act as a magnet.

From the outset it was obvious that these matters would take many years to resolve and be extremely costly. Plans for new deep drainage schemes, one for East Hull and one for the West, were worked on by the City Engineer's staff during the 1930s but interrupted by other priorities as soon as war began. Afterwards however the East Hull scheme, urged forward by political pressure, was soon to get under way and sufficient progress was made to permit house-building to begin at Bilton Grange by 1950 (*see page 7*).

The West Hull scheme, planned and financed jointly by Hull Corporation and Haltemprice Urban District Council, followed on 26th May 1950 when Councillor J.S. Wilson (chairman of the joint committee set up to supervise it) ceremonially drove the first trench pile to inaugurate work on the river outfall pipe. It proved to be a most complex project and, beset with difficulties such as shortages of steel and machinery, proceeded at a much slower pace than envisaged.

Its key component was the massive Humberside Pumping Station at the corner of West Dock Avenue and Goulton Street, believed to be the largest of its kind in Europe. Construction involved knocking down 38 old houses and excavating a huge sump 60 ft. deep, lined with steel reinforced concrete and 360,000 engineering bricks, in which to collect and screen the contents of the city's drains before raising them by pump for discharge into the Humber. A mix of diesel and electrically powered pumps capable of discharging the maximum flow likely - 450,000 gallons a minute - was provided for. When completed, the old West District Pumping Station in Harrow Street with its 100 ft. chimney and three faithful steam engines (the last ones manufactured by James Watt & Co. of Birmingham remaining in regular use) was phased out and during 1958 demolished.

Feeding into the new station were two deep branch sewers, under construction between 1951 and 1961, one from the Dairycoates direction draining much of West Hull, Hessle, Anlaby and Willerby; the other from Hall Road absorbing flows from North Hull and Cottingham as well as intercepting the waters of three open drains - Setting Dike, Cottingham Drain and Cottingham & Newland Beck - allowing them to be abandoned and filled in. The total area served was 11,220 acres (housing a projected population of 250,000) plus 8,400 acres of farmland between the Wolds and the River Hull.

On completion in 1961 the scheme had cost the ratepayers £4¾ millions. But it had made possible the building of three large housing estates (Boothferry, Orchard Park and Bricknell Avenue [phase 2]) and enabled many more of Hull's citizens to enjoy a healthier, safer way of life.

Patrons wait outside the Palace Theatre on Anlaby Road for their favourite stars to arrive. The Palace remained a popular night spot, even after the old time music hall shows faded away. With a 'Continental' theme, it turned to dancing and cabaret to draw the crowds. Photograph by courtesy of Innes Studios, Hessle.

1958

The year that:-

The Campaign for Nuclear Disarmament was launched and Michael Foot led its first Aldermaston protest march.

Seven Manchester United footballers died in the Munich air crash.

Chi Chi the giant panda came to London Zoo.

The first life peers were named.

The US Pioneer space rocket was launched but failed to reach the moon.

Work started on the Forth road bridge, to be the largest suspension bridge in Europe.

There were race riots in Notting Hill.

JANUARY.

15th Nuclear energy was a major preoccupation of scientists during the 'fifties and to cater for the demand Hull College of Technology began to offer courses for graduates from industry and the local councils. To avoid having to send to Harwell Research Establishment for radio active isotopes, the College even maintained its own 'atomic pile', in a specially screened off area marked with warning notices, behind the Park Street building.

Two massive cold stores, catering for the latest developments in the local fish processing industry, were nearing completion in the Walcott Street area. The first, sponsored by Andrew Johnson Knudtzon Ltd. (a subsidiary of J. Marr & Son) and Christian Salvesen & Co., was to be a 'common store' for shared use by the fish trade and other food firms. It was designed to hold 2,000 tons of stock at a constant temperature of -20ºF. The other was being built for the Eskimo Group at a cost of £120,000.

The latest trawler to be built at Beverley for Newington Steam Trawlers, *Joseph Conrad*, was the last new coal-burning vessel to join the Hull fishing fleet. By the end of the decade, after a programme of conversions to diesel or diesel-electric power, only seven 'steamers' remained based at the port.

FEBRUARY.

6th **The Oriental**, a Bass Worthington public house, opened in Hedon Road opposite the site of its bombed predecessor.

16th The stars of the BBC's 'Six Five Special' - Kenny Baker, Don Lang, Mike and Bernie Winters, Joe [Mr. Piano] Henderson, Rosemary Squires, Carl Barriteau and Jimmy Jackson's skiffle group - made their first appearance in Hull at the Regal.

18th A group of businessmen met at Hammonds Restaurant and agreed to form a Jameson Street Association with the object of making Hull's best known shopping street a magnet for shoppers from near and far. Financed by subscriptions, they planned to mount joint advertising campaigns, arrange street decorations and meet to discuss mutual problems.

Five hundred signatures were collected on a petition headed 'Make the New Theatre your own' after Mr. Peppino Santangelo, theatre director and leading personality in Hull's cultural life, announced that he was retiring in April to live in his native Guernsey. A musician by profession and superb administrator, he had come to Hull in 1933 and rescued the Little Theatre (a pioneer in the repertory movement) from financial troubles, making it one of the most successful in the country. On his departure Whitehall Theatres Ltd. intended to put the 'New' up for sale and it was feared this might spell the end of professional theatre in the city. All kinds of wild rumours circulated including one that it was to be converted into a block of flats. The petitioners, who included members of Hull Playgoers Society, planned to approach the Corporation for help. Mr. Wm. Sharpe took over as manager in April.

Hull's mental health services took an important step forward with the opening of an **Adult Occupation Centre** in Froghall Lane. Users of the the old George Yard centre gained better facilities for crafts and, for the first time, the chance to do outdoor work such as agriculture and gardening. Before centres like this many mentally handicapped people had little alternative but to sit at home just staring out of the window.

The Ministry congratulated Hull Corporation's Welfare Services on being the first in Britain to empty their former Poor Law institutions and house the residents in modern old people's homes.

The last residents moved out of Western General to Wensley Lodge at Hessle this month.

Hull's old-established dawn fruit and vegetable market, held every Tuesday and Friday at Corporation Field in Park Street, was about to be displaced for development. A traditional gathering ground for rallies, public meetings and at one time events such as Hull Fair, the Field was earmarked to take Northern Dairies Ltd. from Campbell Street and a GPO sorting office. The market was offered a pitch on Waterhouse Lane car park.

MARCH.

17th   One of the BBC's popular Brains Trusts was held at the City Hall chaired by McDonald Hobley. On the panel were Hull MP Mark Hewitson, W.J. Brown (ex-MP), Ted Kavanage (TV personality and 'ITMA' scriptwriter) and Hugo O'Hear (economist). An 11 year old Hymers boy asked 'Is there something wrong when a teenage pop singer can earn more than a Prime Minister?'

19th   Legendary rock and roll stars Buddy Holly and the Crickets, whose noted songs included 'That'll be the day' and 'Peggy Sue', played at the Regal during their UK tour. A support artiste was Des O'Connor.

As an experiment the War Damaged Sites Committee decided to place a timber shelter at the corner of Holderness Road and Buckingham Street where the elderly folk of the district could sit and meet for a chat. It was such a success that many similar shelters were erected throughout the city over the next few years.

APRIL.

7th   History was made on Anlaby Road when the Palace Theatre, which had closed in March as an orthodox variety theatre, reopened as Britain's first Continental Music Hall. The old-time shows had been hit by competition from the clubs and television and in response manager Harold Clarke devised a package of changes:
- Removing the orchestra pit and tip-up seats,
- placing the orchestra at the back of the stage,
- levelling the floor to make way for tables with red crush velour chairs, and
- providing additional refreshment bars.
The radical new look introduced by architects Williams, Sleight & Co. gave the place a continental café atmosphere. For 2/6 patrons could enjoy a night of continuous entertainment, dance to Harry Chatterton & His Continentals and watch a variety of acts compered by Hull-born comedy star Freddie Sales while partaking of a light meal. The progress of the venture was watched with keen interest throughout the country.

17th   Under Government plans to reorganise the army it was announced that the East Yorkshire Regiment, which recruited from the Hull area, would be merging in 1959 with the West Yorkshires under the title 'Prince of Wales Own Regiment of Yorkshire.' Until a new central base was built the Victoria Barracks at Beverley would remain their regimental home. Meanwhile the last regular army unit in the city - H.Q. Movement Control, North-East Ports - was closing down. Once 250 strong it had controlled the dispatch of war stores and equipment on the docks from a base at Riverside Quay.

Myton Primary School at the corner of William Street and Porter Street, the first new city centre school since World War I, was completed. It was designed on an open-plan layout by the City Architect and built by the City Engineer, with extra large windows to allow plenty of light to penetrate the enclosed site. The school offered 250 places for children drawn from the resurgent housing area at the eastern end of Hessle Road.

MAY.

6th   A 149 ft. high tower-crane that began to hoist girders into place on the College of Technology site was the first of its kind to be seen in Hull.

20th   Watched by thousands of black and white scarved youngsters waving flags, the victorious Hull F.C. Rugby team toured the city in a coach to show off the Rugby League Championship Cup they had brought back from Odsal after beating Workington Town in the final by 20 points to 3. The Airlie Birds had finished the season in fourth place in the league.

27th   Over 450 people turned up to hear the Archbishop of York, Dr. M. Ramsey, consecrate the **Church of the Ascension** in Calvert Road. The building had been adapted from a dual-purpose school hall/church at a cost of £20,000. The pews came from the redundant Christ Church and the altar plate from St. James. The bell, once the Mariners Bell of Hull, dated from 1667 but the oldest feature was an 18-stone block of red marble brought from Iona in Scotland. With St. Thomas's recently completed, it was the only parish in England to get two new churches within a year.

The 'fifties young generation enjoying an evening of Rock 'n' Roll at the Continental and perhaps a brief chance to appear on television when the BBC's 'Six-Five Special' came to town. Photograph by courtesy of Innes Studios, Hessle.

Someone coined the nickname 'Old Men's Parliaments' for Corporation shelters like this one at Chanterlands Avenue because they provided a place where the elderly folk of the district could meet up for a chat and put the world to rights! Photograph by courtesy of Hull City Council Department of Planning and Design.

30th **Zimmerman's Cash Furnishing Stores**, previously in Ferensway, opened at 57 Paragon Street in new premises on the site of S.P. Wood's ironmongery store. At a time of national shortages the building was specially designed by Mr. R.G. Clark to make minimal use of materials. The frontage featured 'Wallspan' curtain walling with coloured glass panels below the windows to eliminate the need for painting.

The Markets & Abattoirs Committee called for an end to the practice of driving cattle 'on the hoof' through the streets of Hull following a serious hold up of road traffic during the mid-day peak one day earlier in the year. To save on heavy railway charges livestock being exported by shippers T.E. Kettlewell & Son was driven from Kingston Street Goods Yard through the Old Town to the lairage on Victoria Dock, an operation that took 30-35 minutes and caused motorists to fume. The Chief Constable described the practice as 'completely behind the times' in a big city and feared even worse chaos would arise when Drypool Bridge was being rebuilt.

There was dismay when the latest trade figures showed Hull slipping to fourth place in the 'league table' of British ports, behind Manchester. Traditionally only London and Liverpool handled a greater value of cargoes. A conference was called to look into the matter and it was thought that Hull's dock charges, slow turn-round times and inadequate facilities, especially for handling grain, were losing it trade.

JUNE.

3rd Work started on replacing the timber decking of North Bridge with a new aluminium-alloy deck surfaced with asphalt, to get it into pristine condition to take the extra load expected with next year's closure of Drypool Bridge.

4th The new Ellerman's Wilson Line passenger/cargo ferry mv. *Bolton Abbey* set sail on her maiden voyage to Rotterdam, knocking four hours off the passage time of her 48-year old predecessor the ss. *Bury*.

12th The tiny **Station public house** in Ferensway, better known to its regulars as the 'Old Dublin', closed its doors. Former licensee Mrs Edith Dyer came out of retirement to pull the last pint and more than a thousand customers from all over the county called in during the day for a farewell drink. Demolition of the inn and the old Zimmermans store surrounding it began the next day.

14th Another new church to be consecrated by the Archbishop of York was **St. Michael's & All Angels, Orchard Park Road**. Designed by Mr. F.F. Johnson its plain elevations concealed a light, spacious and highly decorative interior with the traditional ecclesiastical brown being discarded in favour of modern blues, greys and pinks. A mural by Dennis Booth symbolised the theme of life given by God and offered back in worship. The 800 year old font came from the deserted village of Wharram Percy and the organ from Promenade Chapel, Bridlington. Standing beside the original dual-purpose building given by Mr. R.G. Tarran the church now assumed full parish status in an area about to witness a marked population growth.

20th Mr. Clifford Dunn, a market trader who was on the brink of revolutionising shopping habits by pioneering cut-price supermarkets, opened a store called **'Savemore'** in the Market Place.

23rd Demolition of the enormous **Jubilee Methodist Church** on Spring Bank began. The 1,100 seat Italian-style building, dating from 1863, was in constant need of repair and badly affected by vibration from passing traffic. Running costs were so high that it was decided to replace it with a smaller building. In the meantime the Sunday school in Freehold Street was licensed for services, the congregation joining with the Fountain Road Methodists whose church had been bombed.

There were plans to name a road after the Finnish composer Jan Sibelius in recognition of Hull's shipping contacts with Finland. Eventually the Works Committee decided to give all the streets on the new Boothferry Estate North a musical theme.

On Hedon Road work was about to begin on a factory for **Electro-Furnace Products Ltd.**, to produce abrasives from bauxite. The firm planned to create 100-125 jobs.

JULY.

8th A planning inquiry opened at County Hall, Beverley into proposals by Mr. Harold Needler and Hull Corporation to build houses on land they owned north of Sutton Road outside the city boundary. Mr. Needler had wanted to build a 'garden village' there in 1939 but the site was later requisitioned for temporary housing. Hull Corporation (faced with a need to house 26,000 people on 'overspill' land by 1971) planned a 260 acre residential estate with a further 158 acres for schools, public open space, a sewage works and service industry between the River Hull and the Foredyke Stream. In March 1959 the Minister rejected the separate schemes but paved the way for further talks with a view to the comprehensive development of the area now known as Bransholme.

22nd   Alderman F. Holmes cut a tape to bring into use an inner-city sports ground that had been transformed from waste land behind the College of Commerce in Brunswick Avenue. It had been laid out with tennis courts, netball pitches, a basketball court and practice cricket pitches for the benefit of local sports clubs and schools without grounds of their own.

27th   Hull Corporation Transport introduced one-man operated cross-city bus services 1 and 2 linking Gipsyville and Marfleet at hourly intervals on Saturdays and Sundays only.

The demolition of John A. Scott's No.11 warehouse to make way for a 45 ft. wide approach road marked the first stage in the plan to replace **Drypool Bridge**.

Vehicles with a new style of registration plate were starting to appear on Hull streets. All the three-letter plates in the sequence AAT to YRH had been used up and so a new series of four numbers followed by KH was devised.

AUGUST.

11th   The new factory of **Priestman Bros. Ltd.** on Hedon Road was completed.

15th   Damage was caused to more than fifty big plate glass windows at Hammonds, Thornton Varley's, Bladons and the North Eastern Gas Board during the night by someone with a glass cutter or diamond. £1,000 worth of damage was caused at one store alone.

16th   In an effort to speed up refuse collecting and make it a less dusty operation the Corporation introduced a new £4,000 high-tech dustcart, the forerunner of many more. It had long revolving propellers to draw in and compress the rubbish and was capable of storing nearly three times as much as the old side-loading type.

21st   Bilton Grange's first public house, the **Flower Pot** on Staveley Road, was officially opened by Miss Carrie Jones, a barmaid at the Royal Flower Pot in Whitefriargate until its closure on the same day in 1922. The old pub had been a sailor's haunt and two dozen of its regulars met up again to relive memories. Each received an inscribed

tankard and Miss Jones was presented with a key by Col. C.H.S. Cooper, managing director of Hull Brewery Co. Ltd. The new inn was designed by Messrs. Priestman & Lazenby and built by F. Pape of Beverley.

26th   The first sea-going ship to be built in Hull since the closure of Earles Yard in 1931 was launched from the dock basin of Drypool Engineering & Dry Dock Ltd. by Mrs V.M.E. Rowbotham, wife of the company chairman. The vessel - the 1,000 ton coastal tanker *Oarsman* - did not slide down the customary slipway. Instead the waters of the River Hull were gradually allowed to flood the dock until she rose from her cradle and Mrs Rowbotham stepped forward to cast the champagne bottle. The dry dock had been converted from a lockpit at the old entrance to Queens Dock.

The steeple of St. Paul's Church, Sculcoates was being dismantled because the after-effects of war damage had rendered it unsafe.

SEPTEMBER.

1st   As the nation's premier fishing port Hull stood to be seriously affected when Iceland introduced regulations to extend her fishing limits from four to 12 miles. It was the second time in six years that an extension had been imposed unilaterally and Britain, together with other European nations, refused to accept the decree by claiming historical rights. This led to the first of the bitter conflicts referred to as Cod Wars. Despite harassment from the Icelandic coastguard vessels *Odin* and *Thor*, Hull trawlers carried on fishing the disputed waters for 2½ years, working in 'boxes' under Royal Navy protection.

6th   Traffic lights were brought into operation to control the busy junction of Holderness Road and Ings Road.

10th   Hull's first municipal indoor flower show, the idea of Parks Committee Chairman Alderman Kneeshaw, took place at the City Hall. It was modelled on the club shows run by the Hull & E.R. Crysanthemum Society, the cactus and carnation societies and the Townswomen's Guild who combined to make it a joint success. Despite the poor growing season nearly 1,000 exhibits competed in 157 classes for 39 cups and trophies and £200 in prize money. Besides flowers, vegetables and trade stands there were excellent displays of cakes, bread, home-made jam, bottled fruit, honey and tropical fish. The plan was to put Hull on a par with other cities that already ran Council-sponsored events.

Both Wm. Jackson & Son Ltd. with 36 grocery branches, and Wm. Cussons Ltd. with 30, enjoyed the widespread support of housewives in the 'fifties ...

1950s SHOPPING

... however, food was just as likely to be bought from a 'corner shop' like this one in Harley Street.

Photographs by courtesy of Hull City Council Department of Planning and Design.

Always popular with Hull shoppers, W. Boyes & Co. first came to Hull in 1920, buying up Johnny Wardell's store in Hessle Road. A view of their original premises, before they were entirely rebuilt and extended in 1957. Photograph by courtesy of Sam Allon Collection.

Local booksellers and stationers, A. Brown & Sons Ltd. moved to George Street in 1956. Their 'walk round' window display was typical of that era. Photograph by courtesy of Hull City Council Department of Planning & Design.

13th A ceremony was held to mark the completion of the new **Derringham Bank Methodist Church**, a prominent landmark in West Hull. It was designed for 400 worshippers by Messrs. B. Blanchard and G.D. Frankish in a contemporary style and built by F. Sewell & Son. The £40,000 cost was financed largely from war damage payments awarded to the abandoned Coltman Street Church in whose memory a meeting room was named. With 300 members Derringham Bank was one of the strongest Methodist societies in the North of England.

19th Hull's long-awaited **Central Ambulance Station** in Osborne Street was officially opened by the High Steward Mr. H.S. Morrison. Building had been set back for over a year by a Government spending squeeze. The station cost £70,000 and was designed to service 45 vehicles currently housed in delapidated sheds in Scarborough Street and Waterloo Street. Its nerve centre was the control room where the chief officer could be in radio contact with every ambulance on duty in any part of Hull. Emergency calls were relayed by direct line from the Central Police Station. The opening speeches were drowned by traffic noise because a trade dispute with the plumbers had delayed the completion of glazing work!

OCTOBER.

4th   HRH The Princess Royal came to lay a foundation stone for the soon-to-be-reconstructed church of **St. Columba, Holderness Road**, 32 years after performing the same duty for the original church which fell in Hull's last big air raid on 13th/14th July 1943. Some of the surviving arches and walls were to be incorporated in the new building which was required by the town planners to stand several feet back from its old position to allow for the future widening of Holderness Road.

14th   Extensions to Hymers College to provide new science laboratories and a School Block on a site previously occupied by temporary buildings were opened by Lord Middleton.

20th   Something new on the local scene was a Chinese restaurant. At the Hoi Sun, 47 Jameson Street, Chinese chef Mr. Li Kau and his 13 staff were offering a three-course lunch for 3/6d. and a choice of 97 Chinese and English dishes. A fortnight later the Red Lion Chinese Restaurant opened above Fletchers store and several more quickly followed.

26th   The new southern extension to **Ferensway** beside the Cecil Cinema was fully opened to traffic. Midland Street, for years a troublesome bottleneck for Hessle Road traffic, was made one-way in a southerly direction and the inward no. 70 trolleybuses were re-routed via the new road. Although Government sanction only permitted a 22 ft. wide road initially, there were plans to create a dual carriageway by demolishing the terrace houses in Trinity Square and to extend it to join the proposed South Orbital Road at Myton Place as soon as funds allowed.

NOVEMBER.

21st   There was a burst of new shop openings in the city. Teals furniture store at the corner of Newland Avenue and De Grey Street, designed by Mr. Rowland Herbert and built by Stan Spruit, was opened by the Lord Mayor. At 418-20 Hessle Road Cattles launched a furnishing store while on Longhill Estate a Carlines Cash and Carry supermarket (the 28th in an ever-expanding chain) was launched by Ron Parry, compere at the Continental. It was part of a neighbourhood centre being developed in Shannon Road along similar lines to the one on Bilton Grange. In 1958 the store's policy of staying open until 8 p.m. on Fridays was quite a novelty.

26th   A new Christmas lighting scheme in Jameson Street was switched on at 8 p.m. by Miss Dorothy Rowlands, the 'Jameson Street Queen' chosen from 65 competitors at the first dance of the recently-formed Jameson Street Association. A crowd of 10,000 packed the street for the ceremony while the R.A.S.C. Band played and the Hull Co-operative Choir sang. When it was announced in September the lighting scheme promised to be one of the brightest and most attractive in the country, aiming to rival London's Regent Street. The Association acquired set-pieces from the seaside towns of Ramsgate and Broadstairs to illuminate the 1,200 ft. long street including Cinderella's coach, boxing cats, a giraffe, a Viking ship and hundreds of fairy lights erected free of charge by the Corporation. Special trains and buses were planned to bring visitors from neighbouring towns and villages. The next night it was the turn of Paragon Street to be lit up, a 3,000-strong crowd watching Sigrid Bellamy (a nine year old schoolgirl in Norwegian costume) flick the switch. It was the first year that the gift Christmas tree from Scandinavia had stood in Paragon Street instead of Queens Gardens. Illuminated models of nursery rhyme characters graced the flower beds and even the telephone boxes caught the festive spirit, topped with giant imitation dials bearing a 'Merry Xmas' greeting.

29th   British Railways completely closed the former Hull & Barnsley line west of Little Weighton in a bid to save money, the final coal train being hauled into Springhead Yard by steam

During 1958 Ferensway was extended southwards alongside the Cecil Cinema to connect with Osborne Street, affording Hessle Road traffic more convenient access to the city centre. It was the first new road scheme to be completed since the war. Photograph by courtesy of Hull City Record Office.

locomotive no. 90352. The track, which practically duplicated the main line into the city from West Yorkshire, had in recent times been used exclusively for freight traffic, mainly coal for shipment from Alexandra and King George Docks, a trade which was in severe decline. Despite protests from Hull Corporation and others that the line would be needed if the export trade revived the closure was finalised on 6th April, 1959 leaving only a pick-up goods serving Willerby and Little Weighton.

Workmen were busy reconstructing the retaining walls of the old Horse Wash at the Pier with sheet piles and concrete.

DECEMBER.

2nd   A big blaze destroyed an upper floor and almost all the roof of King & Co.'s hardware showrooms in South Church Side during the afternoon.

10th   Fire flashed through a second floor department of Smith & Nephew Ltd.'s Neptune Street factory late at night causing thousands

industrial tapes.   Fortunately 30 firemen with eight appliances managed to get the outbreak under control in half an hour and prevent it spreading to other parts of the plant.

16th   At a Town's Meeting held in the City Hall the electors present voted by 140 to 7 in favour of allowing Hull Corporation to seek powers to erect a bridge over the Humber at an estimated cost of £14 million as soon as circumstances permitted. The motion that a Humber Bridge Bill be promoted in the next session of Parliament was proposed by Alderman Fred Holmes, chairman of the Parliamentary & General Purposes Committee and an ardent supporter of the Humber crossing. Despite the strategic importance of the subject matter and its far-reaching financial consequences fewer than 200 citizens bothered to attend the meeting.

Work was under way on two new housing estates: The first part of **Boothferry Estate** to the north of Boothferry Road and a development of 121 homes in the **Lomond Road/Kirklands Road** area.

Jenny's café in Bond Street, a popular 'meeting and eating' place particularly for the artistic fraternity. The first floor housed the office of local artist and architect Allanson Hick. Many streets were still illuminated by gas though a programme to convert the 4,500 remaining gas lamps had begun in 1952. Photograph by courtesy of Hull City Council Department of Planning and Design.

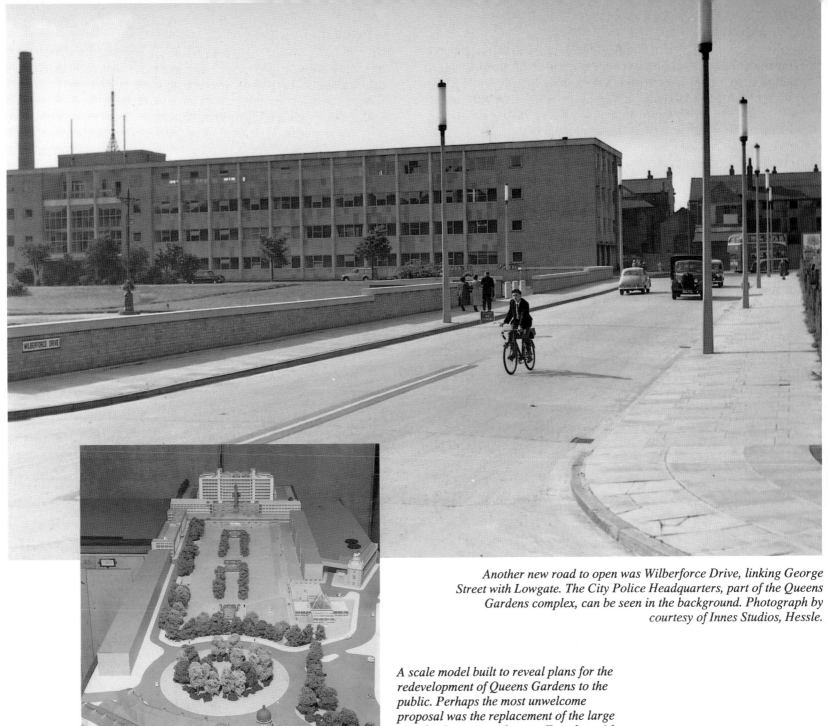

Another new road to open was Wilberforce Drive, linking George Street with Lowgate. The City Police Headquarters, part of the Queens Gardens complex, can be seen in the background. Photograph by courtesy of Innes Studios, Hessle.

A scale model built to reveal plans for the redevelopment of Queens Gardens to the public. Perhaps the most unwelcome proposal was the replacement of the large circular fountain with trees. Together with the 'winter gardens' (seen on the right), the idea was later abandoned. Photograph by courtesy of Innes Studios, Hessle.

A NEW CIVIC CENTRE FOR HULL.

A prime preoccupation of the city fathers in the 1950s was the concept of transforming the Queens Gardens area into 'a civic square of noble proportions'. The intention was to create a public precinct surrounded by dignified and well-planned buildings that would ultimately become one of the most beautiful civic centres in the country - in short a peaceful refuge from those evils of 20th century urban living - noise and speed.

The site of Hull's first dock since 1778 (named Queens Dock in honour of a royal visit in 1854), in its heyday it had been a hive of commercial activity. Passages were booked from here to the Continent and New World and slaves were regularly traded at its auction marts until Wilberforce put paid to this unsavoury practice. By the 1930s however the dock had outlived its usefulness and was bought by the Corporation for £117,000 for the purpose of making an 'open boulevard or town garden'. This bold scheme, inspired by local architect Sir Wm. Alfred Gelder, was completed in 1935 after in-filling by controlled tipping with furnace ash and household refuse. The Wilberforce monument was relocated nearby and the new 'Queens Gardens' with their long avenue of trees and coloured fountain set in a massive roundabout became a feature almost unique in a British city centre.

Shortly after the war the Council chose the eastern end of the gardens as the site for their new College of Technology. A growing awareness of the importance of technical education to modern industry and commerce and the difficulty of administering a burgeoning institution of 500 full-time and 4,000 part-time students scattered about Hull in 17 different annexes made new premises imperative. Simultaneously plans were being made to construct new police headquarters, a custom house, colleges of art and commerce and extensions to the Guildhall.

In the circumstances it seemed sensible to prepare an overall scheme to ensure that the design and elevations of the buildings and the layout of the gardens would be pleasing, harmonious and worthy of their position at the heart of the city. The Council therefore appointed Mr. Frederick Gibberd, an architect and town planner of national eminence, as consultant to advise on all these matters. His initial proposals were approved in April 1956.

The buildings were carefully positioned so as to give what was hitherto a shapeless, windswept and rather neglected open space a welcome sense of enclosure, with the majestic nine-storey college block closing the long vista at one end. In contrast to the neo-Georgian lines chosen for Ferensway and the post-war block developments such as Queens House, a more contemporary style was favoured featuring Portland stonework, golden-brown bricks and panels of glass and green Westmorland slate.

By 1958 the new police building was fully operational; phase one of the college was in place and the second phase rising slowly from its foundations; and a new link road - Wilberforce Drive - was about to open. Later that year the Town Planning Committee approved a £175,000 new look for the gardens themselves, involving:
- Replacing the large fountain with two smaller ones set in lakes, with a further water feature in front of the college,
- Smoothing the undulations caused by haphazard settlement of the in-fill material and laying out fresh lawns at a lower level than before,
- Adding clumps of trees and secluded paved areas with seats and flower beds,
- Building a glass pyramid-shaped Winter Garden housing exotic plants, tropical fish and birds and a small restaurant just opposite Marks & Spencers, and
- Closing Grimston Drive. No roads were to cross the gardens and car parking would have no place in what was to be regarded as 'the gem of the city'.

When a model of the scheme was revealed at Ferens Art Gallery in 1959 it received a mixed public reaction, especially a decision to commission six abstract stone panels for the side walls. The work of Hull sculptor Kenneth Carter, they were said to be 'based in a small way on sea forms'. Those who were not outraged at the spending of £1,200 of public money on them were to say the least a little puzzled as to what they were supposed to be.

To give relief to worsening local unemployment, Government sanction for the project was rushed through and the City Engineer commenced laying foundations in May 1959. The gardens reopened two years later, bringing nearer the fulfilment of the plan to give Hull a civic centre to be proud of. Not all the proposals reached fruition however. The idea of removing the big fountain met with stiff public opposition and was eventually abandoned. Financial pressures meant the winter gardens were never built while the central portion of the northern side, once earmarked for a museum, remained undeveloped at the time of writing.

Work under way at the eastern end of Queens Gardens on the construction of an ornamental pool, early in 1959. Government approval for the project was hurried through to arrest Hull's deteriorating employment situation. Photograph by courtesy of Hull City Record Office.

H.R.H. The Princess Royal walking along Riverside Quay, accompanied by Port Officials, after declaring it fully operational in May 1959. The Quay was important for Hull's near-Continental and Mediterranean perishable trade, which required a fast turnround of ships. Photograph by courtesy of Innes Studios, Hessle.

1959

The year that:-

The Vickers Vanguard turbo-prop airliner set up a Transatlantic flight record - 2,500 miles in 5½ hours.

The Litter Act made it an offence to drop litter.

Five thousand were dead or missing after a typhoon in West Japan.

The Conservatives retained power with a 100 seat overall majority.

There was one of the longest droughts ever recorded in Britain.

The first stretch of the M1 London to Yorkshire motorway opened to traffic.

The hovercraft and Mini Minor car were two new modes of transport.

JANUARY.

3rd   The 8 a.m. 'Bridlington Flyer' special business express pulled into Hull Paragon under steam motive power for the last time.

4th   The **West Park Cinema** was the first in a long line of Hull picture houses to surrender to economic forces and close down (*see page 143*).

16th   After 19 degrees of overnight ground frost, all unloading of timber came to a halt at Victoria Dock because the railway bogies were frozen to the lines under a thick layer of ice.

16th   With 6,250 people out of work (4.6% of the working population), the highest number since the war, Hull's plea for special consideration was finally answered when the Board of Trade agreed to include it in a list of places eligible for grants and assistance to industry. The news came as a relief to the Employment Committee after months of hard campaigning. Grant aid worth £200,000 was awarded immediately so that men from the Labour Exchanges could be set to work converting Holderness High Road into a dual carriageway. Although a welcome move, it was widely recognised that more than short-term relief was required and that Hull badly needed to attract more industry.

The Minister of Housing and Local Government gave Hull Corporation the go-ahead to build houses on land at Anlaby Park Road South. Work had commenced by June.

FEBRUARY.

4th   The Sheriff of Hull officially opened the **Rediffusion headquarters** on Beverley Road after they had been extended to give a total street frontage of 136 ft.

11th   Holmes Tannery in Bankside sustained £50,000 worth of damage in an all-night blaze, Hull's fourth largest post-war conflagration. A six-storey shed and office block were destroyed only months after a previous fire at the premises.

12th   The death of Alderman John Dunbar, chairman of the Welfare Services Committee and good friend of Hull's old folk, occurred at the age of 74. Five days later Mr. Darley, the Director of Welfare Services, also died.

17th   Mr. John Rodgers (Parliamentary Secretary to the Board of Trade) toured some of Hull's unemployment black-spots. He was shown work in progress on the two new **Oil Jetties at Saltend** and the foundations of a £750,000 abrasives factory on Hedon Road. Since designation as an 'assisted area' there had been 30 enquiries for factory sites; work had been accelerated on the **Queens Gardens** project and an earlier starting date agreed for a new **Roman Catholic Grammar School**.

18th   Councillor C.J. Hurley (Housing Committee chairman) laid the foundation stone of the first 12-storey block of flats in Porter Street, part of a £500,000 scheme to house 204 families on which Truscon Ltd. had begun work in October 1958. Ushering in a new age of multi-storey living in a city starved of housing land, they were to be heated by 'coal-less' electric underfloor systems and would incorporate garages and space for cycles.

28th   The dual-purpose church of **St. Margaret of Scotland**, Shannon Road, designed by Messrs. Fisher & Hollingsworth to serve the 2,500 families now living on Longhill Estate, was dedicated by the Archbishop of York. Meanwhile work was starting on an Anglican church for the Greatfield Estate to be known as St.

Hilda's.

Since 1939 the number of cars licensed in Hull had doubled to nearly 40,000. Motorcycles and scooters were especially popular (19,000 compared with 6,600) while commercial vehicles had risen from 5,300 to 11,500. But car ownership lagged behind the rest of Britain: Only 1 in 16 Hull people had a car compared with an average of 1 in 10 nationally.

MARCH.

8th   A peaceful haven was created in the busy city centre when Rev. D.W. Foster dedicated an amenity garden in Alfred Gelder Street next to the White Hart Hotel. Mr. Andrew Carmichael unveiled a public shelter donated by the Salthouse Lane Old Scholars Association, watched by their President, Alderman Arthur Richardson.

22nd In a move to reduce traffic congestion problems in Paragon Square and at Cecil Corner, inward no. 64/68 Holderness Road trolleybuses were re-routed around Chapel Street, Paragon Street and South Street and the terminus was moved from Hammonds to outside the Daily Mail offices.

Demolition men working for Sam Allon's found the old **Civil Defence and C.I.D. Offices** in Queens Gardens to be one of the toughest jobs they had ever tackled. The structure had been built over the basement of the aborted 1930s Central Police Station project and had a 4ft. thick concrete base laced with several hundred tons of old tramlines. Attempts to raze the building, which had been Hull's wartime A.R.P. headquarters, blunted the points of 300 drills every week for nearly six months.

APRIL.

1st   The m.v. *Bolton Abbey* became the first vessel since the blitz to use Hull's Riverside Quay when she moved from Albert Dock to the newly-completed 'A' berth to load up for the 6 p.m. sailing to Rotterdam. The occasion marked the start of Associated Humber Lines' new timetable of three sailings a week each way operated by the *Bolton Abbey* and her sister ship the *Melrose Abbey*. The latter, A.H.L.'s latest flagship, had made her maiden voyage in January after delivery from a Lowestoft shipyard. Her 1929 namesake was put up for sale and later sailed away to become a Greek cruise ship plying the Mediterranean Sea.

30th   A stormy public meeting took place at Ashwell Junior School to discuss a long-festering dispute between the Corporation's Health Committee and local doctors over surgery provision on the new Greatfield estate. The Corporation had plans for a health centre near Horbury Avenue to serve both Greatfield and the older East Hull housing estate but the G.P.s were threatening to boycott the project, expressing a preference for individual surgeries scattered around the estate. They appeared to regard the centre as an attempt to 'municipalise' the health service and claimed patients would suffer hardship because it was too far away. Surgeries were being held temporarily in Council houses which the Corporation wished to release for family homes. Eventually officials of the Ministry of Health had to be called in to try to break the deadlock.

It was announced that Hull had regained its traditional status as Third Port after two years lagging behind Manchester. Despite the collapse of coal exports over £400 million worth of goods had passed through the docks in 1958.

The anti-aircraft 'ack-ack' gun emplacement at **Costello Playing Fields**, one of the last remaining artillery sites in the area, was being removed. There were angry complaints from householders in the area when blasting broke the windows of their homes. Nearby **Desmond Farmhouse** on Anlaby Park Road was also being pulled down to make way for Boothferry Estate North.

MAY.

9th   Hull F.C. played at Wembley in a thrilling Rugby League Challenge Cup Final. Eleven special trains and numerous buses were laid on to transport an estimated 30,000 fans to the match. It was an exciting end to the decade for Roy Francis, one of the club's most successful coaches, who had piloted the Airlie Birds through several cup competitions but never before to Wembley. Despite a gallant performance, skipper Johnny Whiteley's men failed to lift the trophy, going down 30-13 to Wigan.

12th   The Princess Royal paid a visit to officially open the new **Riverside Quay and Albert Dock reconstruction project**. Ships of many nations berthed in the dock were decorated with colourful flags to greet her arrival at 11.30 a.m. After watching a boat discharging into lighters and seeing fruit coming ashore from the mv. *Bolton Abbey* the Princess walked the full length of the Quay before lunching aboard the mv. *Borodino*. The completion of the Quay was a highlight in Hull's postwar port development. It replaced an old wooden quay opened in 1907 by the North-Eastern

Demolition of the former Civil Defence Headquarters in Queens Gardens during 1959. The walls and base were built of reinforced concrete 3-4 ft. thick and proved highly resistant to destruction. Photograph by courtesy of Sam Allon Collection.

Hull F.C.'s Team for the Wembley Cup Final in 1959. Left to right : Johnny Whiteley (skipper), Bill Drake, Cyril Sykes, Mick Scott, Brian Saville, Brian Cooper, Jim Drake, Arthur Keenan, Stan Cowan, George Matthews, Tommy Finn, Ivor Watts and Tommy Harris. Although returning without the trophy, the occasion did create an exciting finish to the decade for their 30,000 fans. Photograph by courtesy of Innes Studios, Hessle.

Railway Co. which had been totally destroyed by enemy action in 1941. The new facilities included a 1,065 ft. long reinforced concrete quay facing the River Humber, able to take ships at any state of the tide and equipped with three transit sheds and nine semi-portal electric cranes; another quay 1,513 ft. long on the south side of Albert Dock with four more sheds and nine wharf cranes; a modern passenger terminal and new road and rail approaches. The terminal possessed full Customs and immigration facilities and its waiting room was decorated with a splendid mural by Mr. Dennis Booth, depicting river traffic from the Viking long ships to the present day. An 'overhead promenade' along the roof of the sheds continued an ancient public right of way across the site, affording pleasant views of the Humber. Altogether the scheme represented an investment of £1.75 million.

In the afternoon the Princess Royal laid a foundation stone for the **Central Library Extension** in Prospect Street watched by the Lord Mayor, Alderman L. Science (chairman of the Public Libraries Committee). A 3-storey building housing 12,000 books and periodicals was planned, replacing the busy but cramped central lending library. To permit its development alongside, an exchange of sites was arranged with the **St. Andrew's Presbyterian Church**, enabling the church to start rebuilding on the opposite corner of Baker Street in August.

19th   Another long-awaited project finally got under way at 7.27 a.m. when Bridge Foreman Mr. Wm. Hepworth pulled a lever to close the 71 year old **Drypool Bridge** for the last time after an estimated half a million swings. Soon afterwards demolition men armed with acetylene torches started slicing through handrails and girders to begin the eight week job of removing the 400 ton structure. The bridge's 16 ft. road width, which prevented two large commercial vehicles or modern buses passing safely, had created a serious bottleneck on the main A165 route to the docks. The new bridge, designed by the City Engineer, was to be a Scherzer rolling lift bridge like two others in the city. The £617,000 main contract was awarded to Messrs. G. Dew & Co. Ltd. of Oldham. The first foundation pile had been driven at the end of April and a large crane was already in place on the north-west side for moving heavy girders. During the two year building period much disruption to east-west traffic was expected. Bus services were transferred to North Bridge via the new Wilberforce Drive link-road. In an effort to divert docks-bound traffic away from the centre of town new colour coded route indicator discs, an idea suggested by the Junior Chamber of Commerce, were erected around the city's ring roads.

23rd   A 'Grand Reopening' ceremony at **Thornton Hall (St. George's) Methodist Mission** on Hessle Road marked the completion of an £11,000 renovation project to make it one of the most attractive halls in Hull. It had been given a modern foyer, cinema-style tip-up seating, a new pulpit and rostrum, and carpets and decorations in cheerful colours.

27th   Lady Isobel Barnett, TV panellist of 'What's My Line' fame, was at the New York Hotel to launch the East Yorkshire Guild of SPAR grocers, formed to help the family grocer fight back against the growing power of multiple stores and co-ops.

30th   The new **Anlaby Park Methodist Church** was officially opened by one of its oldest members, Miss Ellen Barnaby, to a fanfare of Boys Brigade trumpets. The church was designed by Mr. B. Blanchard and cost £16,800 but thanks to a Buy a Brick campaign and other fund raising efforts it opened almost f9ee of debt.

Hull City clinched promotion to Division II of the football league after winning 19 home games, drawing three and losing only one to end up second in the table.

Four types of private houses were being erected by Stan Spruit Ltd. in Auckland Avenue extension, the prices starting at £2,170.

The Lord Mayor launched a massive publicity campaign to promote Hull as 'Britain's Natural Gateway to the Continent'. 45,000 brochures in nine languages were dispatched around the world in the hope of attracting new trade and industry.

JUNE.

1st   Hull's first three smokeless zones were inaugurated following an introductory Clean Air Exhibition in marquees at Wright Street corner. The Beaver Report (commissioned by the Government after the disastrous 1952 London smog) had described Hull as one of the blackest areas for smoke pollution. To keep the cost down the areas where most homes already had gas points fitted were chosen first, i.e. Longhill and Greatfield and the central area. There were Government grants to help householders convert grates to smokeless fuel and anyone burning coal, wood or paper ran the risk of a £10 fine.

25th   Alderman J.L. Schultz opened the new **North Hull Fire Station** on Clough Road, which replaced temporary hutments at the

By the late-1950s the size and volume of modern road traffic was proving too much for the old Drypool Bridge. The bridge was used by an estimated 10,000 vehicles and 8,000 bicycles on an average weekday and often closed for up to 15 minutes at a time to allow river craft through. Photograph by courtesy of Hull City Record Office.

corner of Beverley Road. The six-engine station embraced all the latest technology including a master switch that simultaneously opened the garage doors, started up the engines of the appliances and turned on the lights, buzzers and warning bells.

29th The Corporation Transport Committee made an historic decision that was about to alter radically the style of public transport in Hull. After receiving a report on operating costs they decided by 6 votes to 3 to draw up a programme for abandoning the trolleybus system and operating all services in future with motorbuses. The proposal caused such a furore when discussed by the City Council that it was referred back for reconsideration three times before eventually being accepted in January 1960. Public opposition was enormous and for months angry letters appeared regularly in the local press, with groups such as the Ratepayers League joining in the battle. To many it was unthinkable that what seemed an efficient and profitable system, using cheap home-produced fuel, should be withdrawn. The facts however told a different story: Since the halcyon days of 1949 the trolleybuses had lost 40% of their passengers compared with 16% for the motorbuses and, with the slum clearance programme now gathering momentum, there was worse to come. Within a few years the heart would be torn out of five of the half-dozen trolleybus routes, the population moving en masse to new estates all lying beyond their outer termini. The cost of extending the overhead wiring to these areas would have been prohibitive. Most of the trolleybus fleet was over 20 years old and the electrical equipment was becoming life-expired. Moreover, diesel buses, possessing greater mobility, were better able to cope with changes to road layouts. In the face of these facts the Committee refused to be shaken. The first route to go was the no. 70 (Hessle Road) in January 1961.

30th The final service was held at **Hessle Road Congregational Church**. House clearance in the area had contributed to a decline in support.

For several weeks the Hull Daily Mail failed to appear in its usual form owing to a dispute in the printing industry. A typed 'emergency bulletin' was issued for 1d. a copy, half the normal price.

JULY.

3rd With the opening of **Tophill Low Pumping Station** on the banks of the River Hull (*see page 70*) the city obtained its water supply from a river source for the first time. It fell to the Health Department to allay public fears about the possibility of dysentry and spots.

4th The recently-completed **Spring Bank Methodist Church** was opened by Mrs Douglas Blatherwick of Newark. Designed by Mr. B.W. Blanchard and built by L.H. Beal on the site of the Jubilee Chapel, it enabled three other societies to close their chapels and come together on one site: Fountain Road (Zion), Argyle Streeet and Alexandra Street Mission.

30th The **Humber Bridge Bill** received the Royal Assent. It was a proud moment for Alderman Fred Holmes who had spent much of his public life campaigning for the project. Since 1867 there had been various proposals to span the Humber with either a bridge or a tunnel but all had come to nothing. With the return of more stable economic conditions in the 1950s public interest revived and it was largely through Hull Corporation and Lindsey County Council keeping up the pressure on MPs that this historic Act came to the statute book. The next step was to establish a 21-member Humber Bridge Board from the interested local authorities, charged with acquiring the necessary land on both banks of the river and then seeking Government sanction for the construction work. How the bridge would be financed had yet to be worked out. A suspension bridge similar to, but larger than, the Forth Road Bridge was envisaged. It was expected to have a major impact on the economic, cultural and community life of the region.

AUGUST.

23rd The sea claimed five more lives when the homeward bound Hull trawler *Staxton Wyke* (H 479) sank off the Hornsea coast after colliding in dense fog with an ore carrier.

24th Wreaths were laid by civic leaders near the Wilberforce Statue in High Street to mark the bicentenary of the great emancipator's birth. The Corporation paid for two more bells to be hung in the belfry at Holy Trinity Church so that a special 12-bell peal, to be known as the Wilberforce Peal, could be rung. Each bell was named after a person connected with the life of the church.

27th The keys were handed over to the occupants of nine bungalows and 18 flats built in an area off Regent Street to be named **Icelandic Close**. Intended for elderly seafarers and their widows, they were part-financed from a £20,000 gift made to the city in 1946 by the trawler owners and main fishing towns of Iceland. It was perhaps ironic that the project came to fruition while Britain was involved in a 'Cod War' against that nation.

Housing conditions old and new, side by side, in Cambridge Terrace off St. Luke's Street. Corporation maisonettes and high-rise flats were gradually replacing the unfit 'sham fours' as the slum clearance programme got into its stride. Photograph by courtesy of Hull City Council Department of Planning and Design.

The railway 'coal cracker', a massive structure at the bottom of Kimberley Street, became obsolete when Botanic Gardens depot ceased servicing steam passenger engines in 1959. Coal was hoisted by the truckload and then tipped into the tenders of locomotives waiting below. Photograph by courtesy of Sam Allon Collection.

Priestman Brothers Ltd., one of several Hull firms to move to Hedon Road where the Corporation had land available for industrial expansion. The Distillers Co. Ltd. chemical plant at Saltend can be seen in the background. Photograph by courtesy of Innes Studios, Hessle.

A man with a dream ... Alderman Frederick Holmes, chairman of Hull Corporation's Development Committee, whose energetic campaigning for a Humber Bridge bore fruit in 1959 when an enabling Act of Parliament received Royal Assent. Photograph by courtesy of Innes Studios, Hessle.

The view along Lister Street was changing radically as workmen finished pulling down the redundant church of **St. James**.

Now that Hull was losing its war scars it was rapidly becoming noted as a 'city of flowers'. The Parks Department made a special effort along the approach roads with 14,000 bedding plants offering a floral welcome at Fiveways roundabout alone. Part of Boothferry Road was being landscaped with grass and trees while in Paragon Street another 14,000 plants surrounded a scale model of the Humber Bridge. The fountain in Queens Gardens was also encircled by a mass of colour.

SEPTEMBER.

2nd   The illness of the Principal Mr. Algernon Wood forced the closure of one of the best known business training colleges in the area, **Woods College** in Spring Bank (founded 1905). Many firms went to Woods for shorthand typists and it had one of the best records for exam. success.

16th   A new type of double-decker bus - with a rear engine and front entrance with platform doors - was on trial with KHCT. Known as the Leyland Atlantean it was destined to become Hull's standard purchase throughout the 1960s and play a major role in the trolleybus replacement programme.

21st   After 21 days without rain, gritting squads had to be called out when the first downpour turned the city's roads into a skid pan.

27th   The dwindling congregation of **Bourne Methodist Church**, Anlaby Road held the final service in their chapel. With many people leaving the area, running costs had become crippling but church officials were reluctant to give up the cause without a fight. To save money it was therefore decided to hold future services in Windsor Hall behind the Perth Hotel.

30th   Lord Rank celebrated the opening of a new office block at **Clarence Mills**, Drypool (where he had held his first job 50 years earlier) by unveiling a plaque commemorating his late father, Joseph Rank the flour miller and public benefactor.

Hull University's 140,000 volume Library was on the move from its cramped home in the science block to a new purpose-built £250,000 building 150 yards away. Since 1955 the library had been in the care of the celebrated writer and poet Philip Arthur Larkin.

Three demolition firms were working flat out to tear down over 400 houses in the **Barnsley Street area** vacated by their residents in favour of newer, more comfortable homes on the eastern estates. It was the latest site to fall under the city's slum clearance programme, begun in 1957 when the Government started offering grants to councils to speed up the removal of unfit property. Hull's programme, approved in 1955, envisaged clearing 15,000 dwellings on a gradual 'worst first' basis by 1971. However, early progress was hampered by the slow rate of housebuilding and the competing claims of the 16,500 on the Corporation's waiting list, many of whom were young couples living with parents awaiting their first home. The doomed houses were mainly 'sham fours' (i.e. living room, kitchen or scullery, two bedrooms and a back yard), often tightly packed in terraced courts at right angles to the street. Most were damp and decayed, had poor sanitation and lacked hot water and bathrooms. 'Blackclocks' (cockroaches) and rats were just two of the everyday hazards encountered by many struggling to raise families in such surroundings. But they were rich in community spirit, a feature not easily re-created in the lower-density modern estates. In West Hull clearance orders had already been issued for property in Cogan, English, Day, Marmaduke, Campbell, Walcott, Selby and Waverley Streets, heralding the demise and eventual dispersal of the Hessle Road fishing community.

OCTOBER.

8th   General Election Day. None of the local seats changed their party 'colours' but in North Hull Mr. J.M. Coulson (Conservative) succeeded Mr. W. Austen Hudson who had retired from the House.

8th   **Park Street Bridge** closed for several weeks to allow the 120 ft. wide wrought iron main span to be replaced with steel girders.

9th   Fifty firemen with 13 appliances fought a big pitwood timber blaze at King George Dock.

14th   Workmen began to demolish the railway coal hoist that towered over the Kimberley Street area, recently rendered obsolete by the changeover to diesel trains. Botanic depot had ceased servicing steam locomotives on 14th June.

16th   Longhill estate's first public house - **the Dart** - was opened by the Hull Brewery Company.

Hull's business and shipping interests welcomed news of a £4.75 million phased improvement scheme for **King George Dock** over the next few years. The main spending was to be on the north side where redundant coaling appliances would be removed and the wharf straightened to provide berths for six large ships. All coal was now passing through Alexandra Dock. There would be additional transit sheds and cranes and a much-needed 50% increase in storage capacity at the grain silo. Work began on 29th December.

The first steps were taken to phase out the Gothic-domed tops used on East Yorkshire double-deck buses, a strange but familiar sight in Hull and the East Riding for the past 25 years. The road level at Beverley Bar, the medieval structure through which the buses were specially designed to pass, was lowered to allow the firm's new flat-topped buses to go through at normal speeds.

NOVEMBER.

11th   Alderman H. Kneeshaw opened a £4,000 pavilion built for the **West Park Veterans** Bowling, Social & Recreation Club.

17th   Citizens were shocked when the death was announced of their Lord Mayor, retired docker Alderman Tom Wray, after a period of ill health. Another City Council member, Alderman Thomas Broadbent, a prominent business personality and founder of Hull Ratepayers League, had also died. He had kept a boot and shoe shop under the City Hall.

27th   'Room at the Top' star Heather Sears opened Girlings fireplace and heating showroom in the recently completed **Tivoli House**, a five-storey shop and office block in Paragon Street designed by Elsworth, Sykes & Partners and built by Messrs. Robinson & Sawdon. The corner unit was occupied by a novel type of snack bar - the **Wimpy Bar** - opening seven days a week until midnight and specialising in 1/6d. hamburgers - 'minced and fried steak sandwiches cooked American-style in front of the customer in 2½ minutes'!

Despite a record shortage of bricks, blamed on a period of exceptional building activity during the prolonged dry spell, four brickworks in the Anlaby Park Road South area were burning out their kilns ready for closure. They included the family businesses of Mrs F. Johnson, Mrs A.M. Ellis and Charles Tune. The land was needed for the expansion of **Boothferry Estate**.

DECEMBER.

11th   A large self-service Co-operative store was one of the first units to open in a neighbourhood centre at **Elm Bridge Parade, Greatfield Estate**. The centre was modelled on those at Bilton Grange and Longhill.

30th   Many Hull streets were suddenly awash, rush hour traffic ground to a halt and families living near the River Hull had to move their belongings upstairs when a freak tide caused the worst flooding in the city for five years. Carpets and furniture were ruined and gangs of workmen and volunteers spent hours clearing mud and silt from the roads.

Three new 'locals' opened their doors: **The Mermaid** (Bethune Avenue), the first in West Hull since the war, named after a man o' war built by a local shipyard; the **Goat & Compasses** (Falkland Road), the first public house at Greatfield and the **Grange** (Hopewell Road), the first in Hull to be run by the Grimsby brewers, Hewitt Bros. Ltd.

Hull Kingston Rovers were seeking permission to build a stadium for 30,000 spectators on a 10 acre site on Holderness High Road. Rovers Chairman Wilf Spaven explained that the 21 year lease was up on Craven Park and the club wanted a ground of their own. A fund of £20,000 had been collected towards the venture.

PRINCIPAL CITIZENS OF KINGSTON UPON HULL.

	Lord Mayor	Sheriff
May 1949-50	Alderman J. Henson	Councillor R.A. Alec-Smith
May 1950-1	Councillor H.J. Barney	Councillor F.L. Bailey
May 1951-2	Alderman R.E. Smith	Councillor L. Rosen
May 1952-3	Councillor A.K. Jacobs	Mr. F.R. Metcalfe
May 1953-4	Alderman A. Richardson	Councillor B. Svenson
May 1954-5	Councillor H.W. Jackson	Mr. A.S. Horsley
May 1955-6	Alderman W. Fox	Councillor W.H. Good
May 1956-7	Alderman H. Kneeshaw	Mr. E.A. Brocklehurst
May 1957-8	Councillor T. Wilcock	Mr. R.F. Payne
May 1958-9	Alderman L. Science	Mr. E.W. Mackman
May 1959	Alderman T.H. Wray	Mr. H.J. Steiger

*Tivoli House, a development of shops and offices
adjacent to the Imperial Hotel in Paragon Street.
Photograph by Harry Cartlidge.*

Patrons queueing outside the Cecil Cinema in 1955 to see Marilyn Monroe and Tom Ewell star in the opening feature 'The Seven Year Itch'. Sadly, crowds like this were soon to prove exceptional despite the plush decor and modern comforts offered by this splendid new entertainment centre. Photograph by courtesy of Innes Studios, Hessle.

The optimism expressed when the Berkeley Cinema opened on Bilton Grange in 1956 evaporated when the new television craze decimated audiences and forced its premature closure. Photograph by courtesy of Messrs. Gelder & Kitchen, Architects.

THE DEMISE OF THE 'FLICKERING SCREEN'.

When Mr. Brinley Evans (managing director of the Hull Cinemas chain) announced that the West Park Cinema was closing on 4th January, 1959 with the loss of 13 jobs, it was passed off as a 'rationalisation' move on account of its proximity to the Carlton further along Anlaby Road.

However it soon became clear that this was the first of many to fall victim to the winds of change sweeping through the entertainments industry. For within two months another four of the city's picture houses had reeled their last film, paid off their staff and locked their doors, namely the Londesborough in West Parade (17th January); the Berkeley, Bilton Grange (25th January); the Priory, Spring Bank West (1st February) and the Eureka, Hessle Road (14th February).

All this was happening in a city which was more cinema-minded than most. A 1955 survey showed Hull to be supporting 25 cinemas with a total of 31,400 seats - one seat for every 9.5 people compared with one for every 11.8 in the North of England generally. Over a three month period the number of admissions totalled a staggering 10,417,000! Clearly many people were in the habit of visiting the pictures several times a week, often occupying the same favourite seat.

By the late 1950s however, a combination of three factors seemed to be working to seal the industry's fate: The impact of TV, especially since the arrival of ITV with its popular light entertainment appeal; the high level of entertainments tax; and pressures on family budgets now that many people had deep hire-purchase commitments after buying domestic applicances they had been unable to get in the austerity years. Cinemas were not suffering alone. Dancing, once the all-consuming passion of most young couples, was also starting to lose its appeal as people opted for more home-based entertainment and shunned 'going out' generally. It just showed how quickly conditions can change to squeeze out a way of life that previously seemed invincible.

The biggest surprise locally was the Berkeley. It had only opened two years earlier after being built at a cost of £112,000 to serve a catchment population on the East Hull estates of over 30,000, twice the figure normally required to make a cinema pay. Mr. Evans, its owner, had been sure it would be a winner. Now the news was greeted with shock and disbelief. The Council (from whom the site was leased) were so concerned that a building of its size might become derelict on a new estate that they set up a sub-committee to consider its future. Alternative uses such as a swimming bath, store and education centre were all explored but to no avail. In the end it briefly and shakily went back to showing films. The Priory, seating 1,258, was one of Hull's biggest cinemas but not even a 600-name protest petition could persuade management that it had a future. By 1961 it had been sold to a London finance company and was destined to become a supermarket.

On 24th October two more suburban cinemas, the Rex (Endike Lane) and Regis (Gipsyville), shut down. They were the first in the ABC chain to close in the city. The Waterloo (Waterloo Street) had also shown its last film, making eight losses within a year.

However the cinema business was not going to go down without a fight. On 15th March the dark clouds were dispelled momentarily when the Regal in Ferensway staged a civic opening for the film version of Rogers & Hammerstein's musical 'South Pacific', the first to be shown on its new Todd-AO system. Structural alterations costing £20,000 were needed to accommodate the system including a new projection box with thousands of pounds worth of equipment and the installation of an extra large, deeply curved screen, designed to make filmgoers feel they were part of the action. The Regal was only the fifth ABC cinema in Britain to be equipped for the new type of film epic which it was hoped would save the industry.

BIBLIOGRAPHY.

The following publications/documents have been consulted in the preparation of this book and, if desired, may provide the reader with further information:

Books.

Allison, K.J. (Ed.). A History of the County of York, East Riding
        Vol.1: The City of Kingston upon Hull.
Bamford, T.W. The University of Hull - The First Fifty Years.
Bennett, Richard. Smith & Nephew 1856-1956.
Boyes, W. & Co. Boyes Stores - The Story of a Family 1891-1991.
Davis, Ralph. Twenty-One and a Half, Bishop Lane (A History of J.H. Fenner &
        Co. Ltd.).
Dickson, Tony. KHCT - A Short History of 90 Years
        Service 1899-1989.
Drewery. G. Bricknell Avenue Methodist Church, Hull:
        Golden Jubilee 1941-1991.
Elton, Chris. Hull City: A Complete Record 1904-89.
Elton, Chris. Hull F.C. & Rovers through 88 Seasons.
Fay, J.B. Wilberforce House: Its History and Collections (1953).
Fowler, Mary. Holderness Road.
Gibbs, I.C. East Yorkshire Motor Services.
Gill, Alec. Hessle Road - A Photographer's View of Hull's
        Trawling Days.
Gill, Alec. Lost Trawlers of Hull.
Gill, Alec & Sargeant, Gary. Village within a City - The Hessle Road Fishing
        Community of Hull.
Goode, C.T. The Railways of East Yorkshire.
Hattersley, R.G. Goodbye to Yorkshire.
Harvey, A.S. The Trinity House of Kingston upon Hull.
Holmes, Frederick. How Your City Council Works:
        The Guildhall and You.
Hoole, K. Railways in Yorkshire: No.2 -The East Riding.
Horsley, Smith & Jewson Ltd. Horsley, Smith & Company 1871-1971.
Kershaw, S.T. Hull Savings Bank 1817-1964.
Markham, John. The Book of Hull.
Markham, John. The Streets of Hull.
Neave, David & Waterson, Edward. Lost Houses of East Yorkshire.
Patrick, George. A Plague on You Sir!
Reckitt, Basil N. The History of Reckitt & Sons Ltd. 1951.
Smith, J.E. One Hundred Years of Co-operation in Hull 1890-1990.
Thompson, Mike. Fish Dock - The Story of St. Andrew's Dock, Hull.
Thompson, Mike. Hull Docklands - An Illustrated History of
        the Port of Hull.
Thompson, Mike. Hull Side-Fishing Trawling Fleet 1946-86.
Ulyatt, M.E. & Dalton, B. Old Faithful: A History of Hull
        Football Club 1865-1987.
Vine, Philip. KHCT 1899-1979.
Watkinson, W.R. Guide to the City & County of Kingston upon Hull.
Wrigglesworth, Edmund. Browns Illustrated Guide to Hull.
Ziegler, Philip. Elizabeth's Britain.

Newspapers, Periodicals, Professional Journals etc.

Architects Journal (2.7.53 and 6.9.56).
Buses Extra (Aug./Sep.1986).
Civic Review.
Hull Daily Mail (numerous issues)
Hull Daily Mail Supplements: The Fifties (3.10.87); Centenary 1885- 1985;
        Cinema City (21.2.87); The Good Old Days (various); The Way We Were
        (various)
Hull Target (formerly Hull Star).
Hull Times Series.
Municipal Journal, The (3.12.54)
Omnibus Magazine, The (May 1963)
Port of Hull Journal.
Select.
Surveyor and Municipal & County Engineer, The (23.5.59)
Yorkshire Life Illustrated (Oct.1957)
Yorkshire Post.
Yorkshire Post Trade Review (Jan. 1955)

Miscellaneous Documents.

Buildings of East Yorkshire, The: Catalogue of Exhibition at
        Victoria Galleries 1965.
Development Plan for the City & County of Kingston upon Hull (1954)
Humberside Connection, The: Humber Bridge Commemorative Handbook.
Kingston upon Hull, The City and County of: Handbook of the
        Development Committee, Hull City Council.
Kingston upon Hull Telephone Department Brochures 1964 and 1970.
Kingston upon Hull Water Department Brochure 1970.
Medical Officer of Health, Annual Report of the (various).

Opening Brochures: Cecil Theatre; College of Technology; Police
        Headquarters; Riley Technical High School
Port of Hull, The. B.T.D.B. Publication.
Reckitt & Colman Ltd. Staff Magazines (1951/1957/1960).
Reconstruction of Drypool Bridge over the River Hull. Article by the City
        Engineer (21.9.60)
Theatres & Cinemas in Hull. Heritage Information Centre Publication.
Town Planning Officer, Annual Report of the (various).
Town Planning Officer: Planning in Action (1959).
Twenty-One Years of Management with the Little and New Theatres in the City
        of Kingston upon Hull (Souvenir Booklet 1954).

INDEX.

Conversion Table for Pre-decimal Money.

6d	-	2½p
1s.0d (1/-)	-	5p
2s. 0d (2/-)	-	10p
5s. 0d (5/-)	-	25p
10s. 0d (10/-)	-	50p